PRAISE FOR REFLECTED IN NATURE

'Whether you have a garden to look at, a flower box or a brick wall, this book is like a window looking out over God's creation wherever you are. The book takes your senses to places near and far to encounter nature as God intended, for it to connect with us, whom he also created. Claire's carefully curated devotions and Jamie's ethereal scripture-encapsulating illustrations are a perfect pairing to complement a quiet time with the Lord.'
Gemma Hunt, CBeebies and *Songs of Praise* **TV presenter and author of modern retellings of Bible stories** *See! Let's Be A Good Friend!* **and** *See! Let's Be ME!*

'In this beautiful book, Claire offers a winsome invitation to us all to notice, to rediscover wonder, and to worship. Here is sumptuous food for the soul. As Annie Dillard says: "We are here to witness the creation… we are here to notice each thing so each thing gets noticed. Otherwise, creation would be playing to an empty house." God is putting on a show. Let's not miss it.'
Jeff Lucas, author, speaker, broadcaster

'Claire Daniel invites us to stroll through the seasons, paying attention to the presence of God in the created world. Her reflections and stories, gently rooted in scripture, offer encouragement and perspective for every season of life. The illustrations by Jamie Poole are a perfect companion – quiet, beautiful, and full of depth. Whether used as a family resource or a personal tool for reflection, this book offers a devotional rhythm that draws the reader into wonder, worship, and rest.'
Leah Boden, author of *Modern Miss Mason* and the 'Tales of Boldness and Faith' series

'What a joy it has been to read *Reflected in Nature*, a beautiful book in every way. With great skill and insight, Claire guides us through the different seasons of the year and helps us notice God in the uniqueness of each passing month. Her love for God, and the created world, bursts from every page. The illustrations are stunning, carefully linked to each chapter. The devotional thoughts are concise and helpful, each introduced by an appropriate scripture. The reflective questions are encouraging yet penetrating, and the prayers seal each chapter with the touch of God. Here is a book to be savoured and treasured, read slowly, and returned to year after year. And of course, bought for others to help them also delight in God.'
Tony Horsfall, retreat leader and author of *Attentive to God*

'*Reflected in Nature* is a wonderful invitation to notice God's presence in the everyday. Claire's reflections are thoughtful and grounded, gently drawing out spiritual truth from the world around us as well as the day-to-day circumstances we face. What especially struck me is the way in which I felt as though I was journeying through different seasons and places in Claire's own life, many of which felt relatable and comforting. Paired with Jamie Poole's striking and unique illustrations, *Reflected in Nature* is a resource to return to in all seasons, offering space to pause, reflect, and realign.'
Naomi Aidoo, author of *Finding Flourishing*, YouVersion Partner and creator of the TIME Framework®

15 The Chambers, Vineyard
Abingdon OX14 3FE
brf.org.uk | +44 (0)1865 319700

Bible Reading Fellowship (BRF) is a charity (233280) and company limited by guarantee (301324), registered in England and Wales

EU Authorised Representative: Easy Access System Europe – Mustamäe tee 50, 10621 Tallinn, Estonia, **gpsr.requests@easproject.com**

ISBN 978 1 80039 370 7
First published 2025
10 9 8 7 6 5 4 3 2 1 0
All rights reserved

Text © Claire Daniel 2025
Illustrations © Jamie Poole 2025
This edition © Bible Reading Fellowship 2025

The author asserts the moral right to be identified as the author of this work

Unless otherwise stated, scripture quotations are taken from The Holy Bible, New International Version® Anglicized, NIV® Copyright © 1979, 1984, 2011 by Biblica, Inc.® Used by permission. All rights reserved worldwide. Scripture quotations marked with the following abbreviations are taken from the versions shown. ESV: The Holy Bible, English Standard Version, published by HarperCollins Publishers, © 2001 Crossway Bibles, a division of Good News Publishers. Used by permission. All rights reserved. MSG: *The Message*, copyright © 1993, 1994, 1995, 1996, 2000, 2001, 2002 by Eugene H. Peterson. Used by permission of NavPress. All rights reserved. Represented by Tyndale House Publishers, Inc. NLT: The Holy Bible, New Living Translation, copyright © 1996, 2004, 2007, 2013. Used by permission of Tyndale House Publishers, Inc., Carol Stream, Illinois 60188. All rights reserved. NCB: Saint Joseph New Catholic Bible® Copyright © 2019 by Catholic Book Publishing Corp. Used with permission. All rights reserved. NKJV: the New King James Version®. Copyright © 1982 by Thomas Nelson. Used by permission. All rights reserved. BSB: The Holy Bible, Berean Standard Bible, BSB is produced in cooperation with Bible Hub, Discovery Bible, OpenBible.com, and the Berean Bible Translation Committee. This text of God's Word has been dedicated to the public domain.

Prayer after Communion (Order One) is © Archbishops' Council 2010. Published by Church House Publishing. Used by permission. **permissions@hymnsam.co.uk**.

A catalogue record for this book is available from the British Library

Printed and bound in the UK by Zenith Media NP4 0DQ

Reflected in Nature
Finding God in the created world

Reflections by Claire Daniel   Illustrations by Jamie Poole

In loving memory of my dad.

Contents

Introduction: Claire Daniel 11

Reflection: Jamie Poole 14

🍃 Autumn

1	A new day dawns	19
2	When bloom fades	23
3	Burning bright	27
4	God knows	31
5	At the heart	35
6	No greater love	39
7	Planting a legacy	43
8	Shining our light	47
9	Peace in surrender	51
10	Preparing for winter	55

Winter

11	Each one unique	61
12	Crown of thorns	65
13	Deeply rooted	69
14	Red, red robin	73
15	Shaping our hearts	77
16	Stargazing	81
17	Swans a-swimming	85
18	Evergreen love	89
19	Working in the waiting	93
20	Spring is coming	97

Spring

21	Hidden beauty	103
22	Busy bees	107
23	Nesting season	111
24	A carpet of bluebells	115
25	In the valley	119

26	Like the weather	123
27	Where my help comes from	127
28	Flowing waters	131
29	Beneath his wings	135
30	Fragrant rain	139

Summer

31	Grains of sand	145
32	Where we are planted	149
33	Breaking waves	153
34	Legend of the sand dollar	157
35	Birdsong	161
36	The passion flower	165
37	Lessons from the butterfly	169
38	Turning towards the Son	173
39	His eye is on the sparrow	177
40	At the close of the day	181

Epilogue 185

Let the heavens rejoice, let the earth be glad;
let the sea resound, and all that is in it.
Let the fields be jubilant, and everything in them;
let all the trees of the forest sing for joy.
Let all creation rejoice before the Lord.
Psalm 96:11–13

Introduction

Claire Daniel

In the summer of 2023, walking among the sunflower fields in France, I felt sad that I had missed them in their full bloom, their tall stems now bowed over. Yet what new beauty there was in this stage: the loss of the vibrant yellow petals revealed the detailed pattern on the 'face' of each flower. In that moment, God ignited a fresh spark of inspiration to pursue a long-held idea of creating a book of illustrated devotionals, exploring how God is revealed in nature. This was further confirmed when the idea took root as the seasons progressed and I visited the Lake District in all its incredible autumnal, glowing hues.

In a way that reflects nature itself, the seeds of inspiration for reflections had been germinating since about 2017. It has been a joyous journey growing the thoughts that God planted in my heart, researching the wonders of the created world and developing them into the meditations that are collected in this book. Like a tended plant, they have changed and flourished, as they unfolded during the changing seasons that brought new inspiration.

I have long been inspired by God's creation: his majesty displayed in the changing colours of each new season. I get such joy from taking photos of nature, in the beauty of every season. Whether it is being awestruck by the power of the sea or marvelling at the minute detail of flowers and insects, immersing ourselves in nature can help us feel a connection with our creator God.

I'm delighted to have had the opportunity to work with BRF Ministries to bring these ideas to fruition, alongside the amazing, inspired artwork that Jamie Poole has created. We see the fingerprint of God all around us – in every leaf that grows, in the birds that fly or in the constantly changing sky above our heads. There is evidence of his glory wherever we look, if we only pause and take the time to see it. Every mountain, river or snowfall reflects the thoughts that God has for us and his care for all he has created. His majesty is on display from the colours of autumn to the fragrance of spring, in the waiting of winter and the warm summer sun, which heats the sand beneath our feet and sparkles on the waves that lap on the shore.

The creator's love and mercy is reflected all around us, in the autumn leaves that fall, showing us that letting go can be beautiful – giving way to new seasons and displays of ever-changing beauty, reminding us that change takes time. There is wonder to be found in each season. I am inspired by views and seeing nature close up and how these can relate to scripture and resonate something of God. The lessons nature teaches us apply in our daily faith walk, in every season of life.

May you meet with God, who is constant and faithful throughout the changing seasons, as you explore these reflections and art. It is my prayer that you will find this book to be a hope-filled companion and a place to meditate on the wonders of God we see in nature, whatever 'season' you are in. Perhaps you will revisit some of the reflections in seasons to come, to encourage and uplift you. May you hear for yourself the whispers of that still, small voice, when you walk in nature or even just step outside for a brief moment, in among the busyness of your day. Take some time to reflect as you ponder on the words and images, recalling afresh those times when nature has made your heart sing and your soul soar, inspiring your own meditation and prayers.

Reflection

Jamie Poole

Nature has always been at the heart of my art. Whether it's the breathtaking landscapes of the British Isles, the crashing waves along a rugged coastline or the tiniest creatures and plants hidden along countryside paths, I find endless inspiration in the world around me. For me, art is not just about capturing what I see – it's about expressing the awe and wonder I feel for creation. That expression comes not only through paint, collage or printmaking, but also through words, which hold just as much power to connect us to the beauty of the natural world.

Since being baptised in 2013, my art has taken on a new dimension. Faith has become a central part of my creative process, and I've found joy in combining scripture with my techniques to create something deeply personal and meaningful. This blend of art and faith has shaped who I am as an artist and continues to guide the work I create.

When Claire Daniel approached me with the idea for this project, I instantly felt a spark. Her vision of highlighting the natural world through the word of God resonated with my own values as both a Christian and an artist. We live in a time when people are becoming more aware of the importance of caring for the planet and understanding our place within it. Illustrating this book felt like a wonderful opportunity to help others connect – with each other, with nature and with our creator.

Of course, every project comes with its challenges. One of the biggest for me was understanding and interpreting Claire's vision in a way that felt true to her message while also staying authentic to my style. But this collaboration has been a joy from start to finish. We share a common purpose: to celebrate God's word and the incredible beauty of his creation. That shared purpose made the process not only rewarding but deeply fulfilling.

This book is a reflection of that journey – a celebration of faith, art and the natural world. It's my hope that the illustrations and words within these pages inspire you to pause, reflect and marvel at the beauty that surrounds us. May it remind you of the connection we all share with each other and with the creator of this amazing world.

Autumn

1

A new day dawns

> The steadfast love of the Lord never ceases; his mercies never come to an end; they are new every morning; great is your faithfulness.
> LAMENTATIONS 3:22–23 (ESV)

I am not naturally an early riser, up with the lark. Despite my intentions to be otherwise, the truth is I am a night owl. However, travel necessity often means that I need to make an early start. It is then that I am rewarded with the most beautiful sunrises, the sky painted in glorious shades of orange, pink and gold, as the sun rises on a new day. The darkness that cloaked the sky is slowly illuminated and shadows are vanquished, as the light of day breaks forth and a fresh day dawns.

Each new day, heralded by the sunrise, brings with it the promise of a new start. When the golden sun breaks through the clouds of early morning, dissipating the gloom and warming the earth, the dew evaporates and a new day begins. A sense of hope and vitality rises with the sun, as a new day unfolds.

We can trust that the God of eternity is also the God who is with us right now, faithful as the sunrise. When we see the present through the lens of eternity, our perspective can change; like a new dawn breaking through the morning mist, we can look for God's kingdom breaking through here on earth.

The rising of the sun brings a clean slate, a clarity that we could not see while the dark of night overwhelmed. Breakthrough is possible, the past is behind us and a day of renewed possibility begins. The morning mist clears to reveal fresh skies and light to carry us through the day ahead. Awaiting us as we enter a new dawn, each day may have its own challenges, but it can also bring joy and change and can hold great potential.

Each day that dawns is different, every time the sky is filled with morning light. Just like our faith journey; as we walk daily with the Lord, we can be renewed and given a fresh start when we bring our lives to him anew. Trepidation may awake with the dawn, as we face difficult days, yet we can know that whatever unfolds God goes with us, his mercies new every morning. With the dawning of each day, we can trust that the one who holds all our days in his hands holds on to us.

 ## Reflect

Spend some time giving thanks for the beauty of a sunrise, remembering perhaps some of the most memorable sunrises you've witnessed, each one distinct from the last.

What sunrise are you waiting for? Where are you looking for new horizons or fresh hope? Or do you simply need the courage to wait for the dawn?

Prayerfully bring to God the events of the previous day. Let go of any hurts or disappointments, acknowledging where you might still need to deal with something that happened, asking for wisdom to know what not to carry into the day ahead.

 ## Pray

Creator God, thank you for every sunrise, the golden orb that burns brilliantly in the morning sky, rising each day in splendour. Chasing away the lingering shadows, it ascends to make its watch over the day. Your word promises that weeping may endure for a night, but joy comes in the morning. When night seems long, help me to remember that morning always comes, with hope for a new beginning. Amen.

2

When bloom fades

> And provide for those who grieve in Zion – to bestow on them a crown of beauty instead of ashes, the oil of joy instead of mourning, and a garment of praise instead of a spirit of despair.
> ISAIAH 61:3

Walking among the sunflower fields in France, towards the end of summer, I was struck by the appearance of these once-vibrant flowers, now bowed over. Taking photographs of them at the end of their bloom, my initial disappointment at missing them flourishing gave way to wonder, as I looked closer and saw a new beauty revealed in this stage.

On the face of each flower, an intricate pattern could now be seen. This marvel of mathematics is an incredible spiral pattern visible when the seed vessels are revealed, after the petals have fallen. The amazing, detailed design of these seed cases was a fascinating reflection of the hand of our creator God in nature. The spiral follows the Fibonacci sequence, where each number in the pattern is the sum of the previous two numbers. The seed pods of the sunflower spiral outwards clockwise and counterclockwise from the middle to the outer edge in pairs of consecutive numbers from the Fibonacci sequence, like 34 and 55, depending on the size of the sunflower. Named after mathematician Leonardo Fibonacci, who discovered this sequence in 1202, it occurs in many other places in nature, with this swirl-of-seeds arrangement allowing maximum capacity.

Broken yet beautiful, these sunflowers are no longer flowering but are still useful, after their glorious petals wilt and fall. Petals like the golden rays of the sun are gone, yet their beautiful, bright yellow vibrancy is only part of their purpose. They may have ceased to be aesthetically attractive, deemed unfit to be displayed in a vase or given in a bouquet, but there are still many uses for the sunflower after blooming. In this later season, the seed pods develop and ripen. These seeds can be collected and used to plant many more sunflowers to harvest the following year. It is truly incredible how many seeds are contained within each flower head, the potential for future growth or other uses including supplying much-needed food for birds or becoming ingredients in many recipes, providing nutritious snacks, sunflower oil or spread.

There is beauty to be found in every season, a harvest to be reaped even when it seems that something is no longer useful or able to bear fruit. Similarly, a single sunflower can provide numerous seeds, proving it still has value and purpose when it appears to have faded. There can be a new beauty in brokenness. Perhaps there is still hope of a long-held dream becoming reality, an answer to prayer still to come or a way to reap a harvest for God, whatever age or stage we are at.

Reflect

Do you find yourself in a season when it feels like the best is over?

Reflect on how God might have a purpose for the time when it seems that the 'bloom' has faded.

What might be the 'hidden beauty' in your current season?

Ask God to reveal the beauty in the ashes for you or someone else known to you.

Pray

Creator God, you have a purpose for every season, even when it feels like there is no hope. Help me to see beauty in the broken, your hand at work in each new season and what you are revealing. Amen.

3

Burning bright

> 'In the same way, let your light shine before others, that they may see your good deeds and glorify your Father in heaven.'
> MATTHEW 5:16

Autumn is a season of change, with the end of summer giving way to new vistas of trees glowing with colour. The red, orange or gold of autumn leaves is incredible to see, illuminated by the sunlight. Burnished with the brightness of warm autumn light, leaves appear gilded with a vibrancy that glows like fire, burning bright with the reflected light of the sun.

The changing colour of leaves is set in motion when the daylight hours and temperatures reduce. The colour transformation, which occurs before autumn leaves fall, is caused by declining chlorophyll in the leaves – the pigment responsible for the absorption of light. Before the leaves begin to drop to the ground – an occurrence known as abscission – carotenoid compounds already present in the leaves, that help with photosynthesis, reveal the vibrant yellow and orange colorations of autumn, as green hues disappear. Oak trees can turn red, brown or russet, while dogwood leaves turn purplish red. Maple trees feature both types of pigmentation, with one colour giving way to the next as autumn progresses and trees enter a dormant state for the long months of winter.

In *The Message* translation of Matthew 5:16, there is the fascinating wording, 'You're here to be light, bringing out the God-colours in the world.' I wonder what this means to you. It indicates perhaps that not only are we called to bring God's light to others but that, in doing so, we can bring out the reflections of God already in the world. Just as green leaves have within them the necessary pigments to become alight with the hues of autumn, the world already has within it the 'colours' of God; evidence of his hand is all around us. Yet it is only revealed when we shine our light upon it. What a challenge, then, not only to go into the world as light bearers but also to bring out the 'colours' of God within others.

Leaves burning bright in the autumn sunlight are a beautiful reminder of the Holy Spirit, the fire that God ignites in us when we invite him to be at work in our lives. Pentecost celebrations take place in many churches at Whitsun, to remember the coming of the Holy Spirit. Crafts and decorations are created, filling these places of worship with vibrant autumnal hues of red, yellow, orange and gold to reflect the fire that was seen above the heads of the gathered apostles of Jesus when the Holy

Spirit descended (retold in Acts 2:3–4). That promised helper Jesus foretold can still set our hearts aglow today, bringing us strength and renewed power to shine light in our world.

Reflect

Where might God have called you to bring his light and colour to?

Reflect on who you know who needs encouraging that they bring colour and light to the world, if they don't see it themselves.

Do others see the 'God-colours' shining in you? Might you need to ask God to reignite the flame of his Holy Spirit in your heart?

Pray

God of glory, you give light to the sun and make the autumn leaves aflame with glorious colour. May I seek to bring out the 'God-colours' in the world, shining with the power of your Holy Spirit at work in me. Help me to reflect the colours of your love to others, burning bright with your love and grace. Amen.

4

God knows

> Trust in the Lord with all your heart and lean not on your own understanding; in all your ways submit to him, and he will make your paths straight.
> PROVERBS 3:5–6

Paths in life can take us on a journey we did not anticipate. Significant events can cause us to stumble or walk a road we would never have chosen. Yet when we look back, we can often reflect on how God directed us. We see, with hindsight, that even in the hardest times he was our constant companion, on the road strewn with brambles of heartache, disappointment or ill health.

There are times when we feel we are stepping into the unknown, walking into an unclear future, or the way ahead seems only darkness. 'The Gate of the Year' is the popular name ascribed to a poem written by Minnie Louise Haskins (1875–1957), published in 1912 and quoted by King George VI in his 1939 Christmas Day address to the British Empire. Originally published with the title 'God Knows', I was astonished to hear my dad recite this poem in its entirety, as I sat with him one night, in his final days. He had learnt this by heart as a child, words so poignant in that moment carrying reassuring hope.

I gave a reading of the poem at my dad's funeral, having prayed him into the hand of God. It is the hope that our imperfect eyes cannot always see – that God knows the path our life will take and what is best, just as he directs each leaf that falls and knows where it will land.

There is such beauty in the falling of a shower of crisp autumnal leaves, watching them cascading down, just as there can be a thrilling freedom in asking God to direct our paths. Uncertainty can rise, as it feels like we are freefalling, yet autumn truly is proof that letting go can be beautiful. It can be a slow swirling fall, like a leaf drifting gently down in an autumn breeze. Yet God knows our destination, and we can be assured that he has a plan for our lives.

When we feel directionless or that the path to answered prayer is far from straight, God asks us to simply entrust our journey into his care. Autumn leaves may appear to float aimlessly, but the destination of each leaf is ordained by God. We can take heart that God knows, when the road we tread is winding, with no end in sight. Charles Spurgeon, influential English Baptist preacher and theologian, wrote encouragingly on this, saying: 'Wherever Jesus may lead us, he goes before us. If we don't know where we are going we know with whom we are going.' Our days are secure in his guiding hands, if we let go of control and place our lives into them.

Reflect

Do you feel like you are drifting on an aimless path, not the one you had planned? Is there something that you have been praying for, and the answer seems to be no nearer to 'landing' on firm ground?

Bring these to God as you reflect on this verse, entrusting them to God, who directs the path of each falling leaf and wants to guide you and those you hold in prayer.

Pray

Unchanging one, help me to put my hand in yours. Stepping into the unknown, it can feel like I'm freefalling, the journey long or aimless. Remind me when my heart is troubled that you direct my path. Help me to trust your leading and recall how you have safely guided me along paths unknown before. Amen.

5

At the heart

> 'The Lord does not look at the things people look at. People look at the outward appearance, but the Lord looks at the heart.'
> 1 SAMUEL 16:7

Searching for conkers with our children has always been such a joyful autumnal activity. The hunt for the fallen bounty of the horse chestnut tree always begins with anticipation – what if they have already all been discovered by other families or turned rotten when laying unseen in the carpet of leaves? We scan the ground hoping to spot shiny conkers nestling among the fallen leaves, pressing gently with a shoe on the unopened, spiky exterior of one still held in its protective casing.

The seeds of the horse chestnut tree are incredibly smooth, in stark contrast to the outer shell. They are commonly known as conkers, a name that is thought to be derived from the French *conque*, meaning conch or shell, or due to its similarity to the term 'conquer', relating to the popular game, where the aim is to knock out the opponent's conker.

Within the sharp exterior, at its heart is a conker as smooth as polished wood. If we don't break through that barbed shell, we would never realise the beauty that lies within. New life and potential lie within this casing, which protects the conker from predators while the seed matures. However, it could not fulfil its purpose if it remained walled in by its guarding, forbidding external layer.

Bitterness or negative experiences can cause us to construct a layer of self-protection around our hearts. Hurts, disappointments and unforgiveness can forge this, like the unyielding shell of a conker. It can keep our hearts from knowing peace, preventing us moving forward and being transformed into the person God has created us to be. When we ask God to break the chains of unforgiveness that weigh us down, we can emerge like the smooth unblemished conker, leaving behind the defensive layer that is no longer needed, casting off that which hinders and free to live unbound.

When we acknowledge the walls that we build up, we must also consider that others we encounter might be concealing a heart that has been hurt or struggling with disappointment or fear behind their outward appearance.

 Reflect

Consider any past hurts or experiences that you might need to relinquish or forgive. Lay your defences down before God, stepping out of your 'shell' that might have been surrounding you for many seasons.

Ask God to open your eyes to see the heart of others as he sees them, past the 'spiky' exterior they present to the world.

 Pray

Gentle Saviour, you see past my walls of protection, and you know the hurts that have hardened my heart. Break through this facade and soften my defences. Help me to see others as you do, to look beyond the outer appearance, to see them through your eyes just as you see to the heart of me. Amen.

6

No greater love

> '**My** command is this: love each other as I have loved you. Greater love has no one than this: to lay down one's life for one's friends.'
> JOHN 15:12–13

We stood in church as our eldest son delivered a reading. It was the first time both our boys were assembling with their respective Scouts and Cubs packs, in the Remembrance Sunday service, and joining the parade to the cenotaph that would follow. Every other sound stilled as we gathered to remember the fallen and those still impacted by war and conflict, and my son's voice was clear as he recited the poem 'The poppy' by D. Rothwell.

Where poppies bloom, their beautiful petals carpet the landscape in a brilliant red. This flower has been the emblem of the Royal British Legion since 1921, inspired by the poem 'In Flanders fields' by John McCrae. Poppies help us to remember the fallen in war and those who continue to give their lives for others across the world in the pursuit of peace – a symbol of hope springing forth after tragedy.

Poppies can also remind us of the blood that was shed when Jesus paid the ultimate price for our freedom, laying down his life that we might know the hope of everlasting life. No greater love than this could we ever know, that conquers death itself through his sacrifice upon the cross. Jesus speaks to his disciples in these verses, his final teaching to his followers containing these well-known words on the ultimate act of selfless love, to lay down one's life for another.

Jesus knew the cross he would bear and the sacrifice he would make for all. Love in action, this unconditional love was freely given and made available to all and for all time. In his farewell discourse, made during the last supper (John 13—17), Jesus prepares the apostles for his imminent departure, encouraging them in the mission set before them, with an emphasis on love, unity and the promise of the Holy Spirit.

No matter how broken, unworthy or unlovable we may feel, the God of the universe surrendered to the grave, to be raised to life, so that *all* may know the greatest love of all. Love that trampled death stretches beyond the grave and opens the gates to glory for all who follow him.

Jesus' words, recounted in John 15, call us to respond. His disciples were yet to see the full meaning of these exhortations, but we read them in the full knowledge of all that followed. We may never be called to put our lives in peril for the sake of others, as those who stand in conflict situations or war. But we can look for ways to live a life of sacrifice, demonstrating the greatest love that Jesus lavished on us, to those we encounter.

Reflect

Consider the places where people continue to take a stand to preserve peace and risk their lives in places of conflict and war. Bring these to God.

Jesus has broken every chain, every stronghold that prevents you from knowing peace and freedom. Spend some time reflecting on this in your life and giving thanks for the sacrifice Jesus made – the greatest love of all.

Pray

Prince of peace, my sin has been wiped clean away by the blood of Jesus. Ransom paid, you faced death to give us life, displaying the greatest love the world has ever known. Help me to remember your sacrifice that opened the way to eternal life. I pray for those who fight to end war and bring peace, past and present. Amen.

7

Planting a legacy

> '*Do not despise these small beginnings, for the Lord rejoices to see the work begin.*'
> ZECHARIAH 4:10 (NLT)

Walking along the shady pathway that skirted a pond, I saw a reflection clear as a mirror, duplicating the 15th-century church, crowned by blue skies. I noticed that the walkway was lined on the other side with oak trees, rustling in the summer breeze, dappled sun patterns dancing across the path where I trod. These oak trees were of many sizes, some quite young and others that had been firmly rooted there for centuries. Each grown from a single acorn. I noticed buds of acorns on some of the branches, the promise of new life to come.

Great things often begin small. It's a cliché, but true, that a mighty oak tree begins as a tiny acorn. Some of our biggest plans start with a fleeting thought, a 'what if…' that takes root and begins to grow. The prophet encourages us in this verse: 'Do not despise these small beginnings, for the Lord rejoices to see the work begin.' Stages of growth matter, each season part of the process of becoming who we are created to be.

Even the most minuscule seeds hold so much potential. They are barely visible, yet they can grow into incredibly intricate plants or mighty trees. However insignificant we think our impact is in the world, do not underestimate the lasting effect our lives and actions can have. The smallest word of encouragement can help someone develop in their faith. We can contribute to the growth of God's kingdom, though we may not always know that we had a part in someone else's testimony.

Acorns take a long time to become mighty oaks, with a tree considered young until it reaches 100 years. Centuries after it is planted, an oak tree can stand 40–80 feet tall, spanning countless generations in human terms. The lasting effect of our prayers or ministering in God's name can make unseen imprints in eternity.

Comparing our achievements or the 'success' of our ministry to that of others can leave us feeling inadequate. Yet there is real strength in the small beginnings we may set in motion. Mother Teresa said, 'Do small things with great love', reminding us never to underestimate the worth of small gestures in someone else's faith journey.

William Arthur Ward, prolific motivational writer of poems and meditations, said: 'Judge each day not by the harvest you reap but by the seeds you plant.' We may not always see the fruition of our labour, but this should not discourage us from spreading the good news of God's love nor leave us with a sense that our time and efforts were spent in vain. We can pray with confidence for the harvest yet to come, though it may be reaped by future generations.

 Reflect

Recall people who were significant in your faith growth. Those who planted or nurtured the seeds of faith in your heart, sharing their wisdom and guidance.

How might you encourage others to persevere in their faith? Is there someone that God brings to mind whom you can nurture or encourage, planting seeds of faith that might one day grow?

 Pray

Mighty God, thank you for those who planted seeds of faith in my life and for their example and guidance. Give me the opportunity to do the same. I may not always see the growth, but I am sowing with confidence for a harvest that can impact future generations. Amen.

8

Shining our light

> The light shines in the darkness, and the darkness has not overcome it.
> JOHN 1:5

Pumpkin carving might be a messy activity, but after scooping out the stringy, seed-laden innards comes the real work: deciding what shapes to carve out. Those all-important gaps allow the light of a candle to pour out of the hollowed-out gourd, when we place them on our doorsteps or driveways.

We have fashioned a range of alternatives to the traditional Halloween pumpkins over the years. My husband takes the prize for his carving technique, having managed to reveal the words 'hope', 'love' and even 'Jesus' around spherical pumpkins. Accomplishing Jesus' name was particularly impressive; the word was on the back of the pumpkin, visible through a large heart in the front, so he had to carve the letters backwards!

It is easy to lose heart when life is dark, but we can be reassured that God is with us. We are called to shine the light of Christ in the world, being a bearer of hope, carrying the light to those who walk in darkness. The light ignited in us by the Holy Spirit is referred to in a beautifully worded prayer, incorporated into the liturgy that can be said after Communion, in the Church of England:

We whom the Spirit lights give light to the world.
Keep us firm in the hope you have set before us,
so we and all your children shall be free,
and the whole earth live to praise your name;
through Christ our Lord. Amen.

May we continue to be drawn to God's light and pray for help to guide others to the light, found in knowing Jesus. We can stand firm in his truth for ourselves and hold the light out to others, as a beacon of hope. Darkness flees at the name of the Lord, and we find in him a hope that can radiate in even the darkest of nights. May we have the courage to step out of the shadows that life can cast and find ways to illuminate the lives of others. It begins with us.

 Reflect

Reflect on ways God has banished the shadows in your life. Look daily for opportunities to share hope with others and to be a light bringer.

Take some time to ask God to strengthen you and enable you to hold on tight to the light, as you seek to share it with others.

Pray

Jesus, light of the world, shadows flee in your name. You take my brokenness and make me whole again, turning darkness into light. Help me to shine with the light of your love that I might bear the light you bring to those around me. Amen.

9

Peace in surrender

> '*P*eace I leave with you; my peace I give you. I do not give to you as the world gives. Do not let your hearts be troubled and do not be afraid.'
> JOHN 14:27

Many years ago, we decided to buy my mother-in-law a potted plant, rather than flowers that would not last. We settled on a peace lily, liking the idea of gifting a plant with such a symbolic name. The *Spathiphyllum* gained its common name of peace lily from its white flowers, which resemble white flags, known widely as a symbol of peace and surrender. This plant has grown with each passing season, now occupying a far larger pot than it arrived in. Ornaments and family photos have been shuffled along gradually to accommodate its wide-reaching leaves.

Naming this reflection 'Peace in surrender' might sound like a contradiction – how can defeat feel peaceful? Meditating on the reason for the peace lily's name, I realised that there is great peace found in surrendering our struggles and asking God to step in. We can know peace when we let go of control, gaining victory over worry or overwhelm, accepting that we do not have to keep battling on alone.

Surrendering to God is not failure; it is freedom. There are times when we cannot overcome in our own strength, and we have to ask God to fight on our behalf. We can lay down our weapons of self-preservation and struggle, hold up our hands and admit we need help, allowing God to carry us to victory. Surrender brings solace in the knowledge that he is in control. It might mean relinquishing long-held unforgiveness or having the courage to admit a wrong. It might require us to lay aside our defences, for God to minister to those places we have not fully laid bare before him. We may need to forgive ourselves or accept the forgiveness received from others, to move forward in victory.

When Horatio Gates Spafford (1828–88) composed the hymn 'It Is Well with My Soul' in 1873, he had experienced unthinkable personal tragedy with the loss of his young son and the family home being reduced to ash by the Great Chicago Fire in 1871. His four daughters perished when their ship sank at sea, with only his wife surviving. Grappling with deep sorrow, he described a 'supernatural' peace that surrounded him and penned the words:

When peace, like a river, attendeth my way,
When sorrows like sea billows roll;
Whatever my lot, Thou hast taught me to say,
It is well, it is well with my soul.

Peace like a river, which flows freely from God, can surround and uphold us in even the hardest of times. Not peace as the world defines it but unfathomable peace, beyond human understanding, a gift from God for every troubled heart.

Reflect

What might you need to surrender? Are there fears or battles you need to place in God's control. Bring these all before God and lay them down.

Who might you need to forgive to know peace? Perhaps yourself?

Pray

God of peace, give me the courage to surrender, to know that it is not a failure to hold my hands up and relinquish to you the situations I have fought so hard with. Fill my heart with peace in surrender and a knowledge that you are in control. Amen.

10

Preparing for winter

> And my God will meet all your needs according to the riches of his glory in Christ Jesus.
> PHILIPPIANS 4:19

Retreating to a woodland cabin for a January getaway before the school year resumed, we were delighted to have various woodland animals wander up close to the sliding glass door that led outside. It was clear that they were wise to the potential source of sustenance offered by the ever-changing human inhabitants dwelling within. It was wonderful to quietly watch as a deer cautiously ventured towards the patio, having appeared out of the woodland shrubbery – so thrilling to see them at such close quarters. We were also visited daily by the far more confident squirrels, who would scramble up onto the table to see if the supply had been replenished.

No doubt we were one of numerous families who left out provisions for the woodland wildlife week by week. They had a plentiful (if eclectic) array of food laid out and an almost guaranteed location from which to supply their need for food, even in the winter months.

It is well known that in the wild squirrels will usually need to store up food supplies ready for winter. However, they do not simply bury nuts as they find them. There is far more involved in this process of securing and storing provisions for a later season. They use a method called 'scatter hoarding', protecting their food by concealing it in hundreds of different hiding places. Some grey squirrels will shake a nut to test if it contains weevils, eating those ones straight away, as they would spoil in storage – perhaps the root of the idea of someone being a 'bad nut'. Squirrels will even dig fake holes or bury and dig up a nut many times, in order to deceive other animal onlookers. Using a detailed spatial memory and incredible sense of smell, they will usually manage to reclaim up to 80 percent of buried stores.

Collecting and storing produce for the harsh and leaner days of winter is something that happens the world over during seasons of harvest and plenty. When we reflect on the ways that God provides for us, we see that he not only cares about our basic bodily needs but also our finances, our relationships and our spiritual nourishment. We can receive from God a harvest of his richest love, mercy and grace when we call upon his name. God knows our needs before we ask and wants to supply comfort, strength and forgiveness.

 Reflect

Are you storing up the right 'provisions', for the long term, like the squirrel quality-testing each nut?

What can you 'store up' to sustain you during any 'winter' seasons in your faith? Take some time to recall words from others, scripture or cherished messages of encouragement that you can come back to, as a source of help when you need it. You might want to write these in a journal or find a place to store keepsakes.

 Pray

My provider, help me to see you at work even in the 'winter' days, when all feels bleak, trusting you to sustain me. Remind me of words and moments that have encouraged my heart and lifted my spirit, when life feels barren, and to hold on to these in the harder seasons. Amen.

Winter

11

Each one unique

> For you created my inmost being; you knit me together in my mother's womb. I praise you because I am fearfully and wonderfully made; your works are wonderful, I know that full well.
> PSALM 139:13–14

In my work supporting young people, I use images of magnified snowflakes with their distinct patterns when discussing how we are all unique and beautiful in our own way. I ask them to consider the vast number of snowflakes we could count in even the lightest fall of snow – then to imagine the quantity that fall when we experience deep snow or in countries that have year-round snowdrifts as far as the eye can see, yet each snowflake is unique!

In 1885, scientist Wilson Bentley discovered that if he attached his camera to a microscope, he could capture photographs of snowflakes' jewel-like construction, revealing intricate details never seen before. No matter how many he photographed, no two were an exact match. Snowflakes float and fall through different atmospheric conditions that determine their design, as they cascade towards the ground. Moisture levels in the clouds, how water vapour crystalises on to them and the air temperature shape each snowflake differently.

There are some lesser-known one-of-a-kind phenomena seen in nature, such as the unassuming daisy, each flower having a variation in size and petal number, and apples from the same tree. When we examine them more closely, each has a little spark of individuality. No two humans are completely the same either, not even identical twins. We all bear an identifying mark in our fingerprints, the pattern seen in the iris of our eye and, intriguingly, even our toes and tongue have a print that has no duplicate! How incredible that God, who made the entire universe, took the time to make each one of us an entirely new creation and looked at the world and decided it needed you!

We all bring something different to the communities we are part of, making our individual 'mark' in this life. Just as a snowflake cannot create a snowdrift by itself, we are called to unite with others, finding purpose and belonging when we forge links with other believers. We are built up and strengthened by knowing we are part of a collective of Christians, part of something bigger than ourselves in serving God.

Do not underestimate the contribution that you make; even just your presence can be an encouragement to someone, as they see the way that you live your life to God's praise and glory. Like the hidden beauty revealed in each tiny snowflake, God created each of us unique and with a purpose – know that you make a difference and have significance.

 Reflect

Consider how connecting to others in church community brings a further dimension to your faith in a unity of purpose. Just as snowflakes join to make snow, how do you work with others to glorify God?

Consider the 'mark' that you make and how we see God's fingerprint in our lives. What gifts and talents might he be wanting you to use for his glory?

Pray

Wonderful one, you design even the tiniest of snowflakes to be unique, with a purpose. Help me know how I can play my part in the body of Christ, using my gifts to bless others and standing alongside the family of believers. Amen.

12

Crown of thorns

> And then [the soldiers] twisted together a crown of thorns and set it on his head. They put a staff in his right hand. Then they knelt in front of him and mocked him. 'Hail, king of the Jews!' they said.
> MATTHEW 27:29

Advent had just begun when I went along to a ladies' night at church for a wreath-making workshop. Having never made one before, I was intrigued to learn the process involved. I thoroughly enjoyed building up the circlet of seasonal greenery, formed from a series of small bunches carefully wired together, selected from the different branches that we were invited to cut swathes of. With piles of beautiful evergreen branches laid out in abundance before me and secateurs in my gloved hands, I was eager to start.

Circular in design, wreaths symbolise completion and continuous life, signifying the eternal, unending love of God, with no beginning and no end. Historically, wreaths are also connected with triumph. The word 'wreath' stems from the Greek word *stephanos*, meaning 'crown' or 'garland', given to poets, emperors and generals as trophies of recognition. In 1 Corinthians 9:25, Paul uses the analogy of the victorious athletes in ancient Greece, explaining: 'They do it to get a crown that will not last; but we do it to get a crown that will last forever.' The glory of heaven is everlasting.

The presence of ivy in a wreath symbolises faithfulness and loyalty; mistletoe is said to represent love and reconciliation; pine cones speak of new life; the crimson berries represent the blood Christ shed upon the cross; and sharp-edged holly leaves, wrought into a circle, remind us of the crown of thorns that Jesus bore. The Christmas wreath is an emblem of Christ's triumph over death itself, defeating sin through his death and resurrection. The holy one, pure and blameless, was pierced for our transgressions; he took upon him the sins of the world, enduring the crown of thorns for each of us. Because of this sacrifice, we can live in freedom from sin, knowing a source of everlasting hope, strength and comfort in our pain and suffering.

Evergreen boughs keep their vibrant green leaves; even as the season progresses, they reflect powerfully the everlasting love of God. It does not change with the turning of the seasons, remaining steadfast evermore. Love never failing, never growing weary or faltering. Affection that does not cool with the passing of time as the human heart can.

When a wreath is hung on the door to a home, it reminds us to invite Christ into our home afresh. May we remember, when we see beautiful wreaths adorning homes at Christmas, the enduring love of our Saviour. Hope everlasting, faithful forever and bought at great cost. Love with no end.

Reflect

What suffering or pain do you need to bring to God, something that you are experiencing or for someone known to you?

Reflect on the symbolism of the wreath. Remember this when you see them adorning doors and invite Jesus afresh into your heart and life.

Pray

Holy and everlasting one, when I invite friends and family into my home at Christmas, may I ask you afresh to enter and make your home in my heart. When I see the wreaths hung on doors, remind me again of the one who hung upon the cross, bearing the crown of thorns and making a way for humankind to have eternal life. Amen.

13

Deeply rooted

> Let your roots grow down into him, and let your lives be built on him. Then your faith will grow strong in the truth you were taught, and you will overflow with thankfulness.
> COLOSSIANS 2:7 (NLT)

A stained-glass window at the front of our church, above the altar, is a focal point before the congregation, showing a beautiful, modern depiction of a flourishing tree. It brings to my mind the idea of the tree of life, mentioned in the Bible, which represents the fullness of eternal life. Rendered in striking coloured glass, the window was commissioned to celebrate the opening of the church in a new location, at the heart of the school community. The tree has broad and far-reaching roots that fill the lowest section of the window panels and appear to grow down into bright, cobalt blue water, reminiscent of the metaphor in Psalm 1:3 for the one who delights in the Lord:

> That person is like a tree planted by streams of water, which yields its fruit in season and whose leaf does not wither – whatever they do prospers.

I like to imagine that those roots, strong, deep and wide in their reach, continue to grow deeper than is shown in the confines of the window – like us being called to spread God's love in our community outside of our church. It also serves as a reminder that as Christians we need to remain rooted firmly in our faith. The depth of our roots in God's word gives us strength and a firm foundation, to weather the storms throughout countless seasons.

It takes time and effort for roots to progress deep into the ground and our 'tree' of faith needs nourishment to flourish. We thrive from the input of others in our spiritual growth, fed by the word of God, prayer and time spent in God's presence. Living a life rooted deeply in the strength of God's love brings stability and security and is life-giving. Cultivating daily a faith that is flourishing and rooted in God enables us to be fruitful and spread wide the good news of God's love in our community.

 Reflect

Consider how you can take steps to strengthen your roots, by digging deeper into God's word, praying and asking him to strengthen and uphold you.

Do your roots need to grow deeper or wider to enable you to hold firm in the seasons of challenge or change or reach out to others?

 Pray

My firm foundation, keep me firmly rooted in you, the knowledge of your strength sustaining and upholding me in the tumults of every season. Ground me in your peace and help me to spread my roots deep in your word. Let my roots spread further to those around me to share the strength found in you with others. Amen.

14

Red, red robin

> Therefore, if anyone is in Christ, the new creation has come: the old has gone, the new is here!
> 2 CORINTHIANS 5:17

On a mild Boxing Day, when our boys were much younger, we decided to take a walk down to the local village park for some fresh air. I still remember the joy felt when we encountered a friendly robin, having heard its melody coming from the shrubbery near the swings. It was clearly used to visitors to the playground and wasn't scared off by our arrival. Quite the opposite, it greeted us with joy! Much to our delight, it flew down from the bushes and hopped along the path, venturing close to where we stood.

Robins, with their famous vibrant red breast, sing sweetly almost all year round. They convey a sense of hope in the depth of winter. Often depicted on Christmas cards, a tradition that began in Victorian times, robins feature in snowy scenes, sitting atop post boxes or with an envelope held in their beak, bearing as they do a similarity to the bright red uniforms worn by Royal Mail delivery staff. They are a herald of the coming of spring and represent renewal, fresh beginnings and hope.

Stories of how robins came to have their iconic red breast have links to Christianity and folklore from a range of sources. One tale tells of their tiny wings fanning the dying flames of the fire keeping baby Jesus warm, resulting in them scorching their breast. Another asserts that this little bird, known in Welsh folklore as *brou-rhuddyn* ('scorched breast'), was named thus when it sustained injury while delivering water to tormented souls in the fires of purgatory. Irish folk tales hold that the robin was present at the crucifixion, removing a thorn from Jesus' brow, to ease his suffering. Yet another tells of the robin comforting Jesus with his song. In both legends, blood from the crown of thorns stains the bird's chest evermore.

Birds appear often in literature, depicted as symbols of hope and encouragement. The poem '"Hope" is the thing with feathers' by Emily Dickinson (1830–86) describes hope as a bird fragile and small, yet it can endure the worst of situations without asking for anything in return:

'Hope' is the thing with feathers –
That perches in the soul –
And sings the tune without the words –
And never stops – at all –

And sweetest – in the Gale – is heard –

…

Yet – never – in Extremity,
It asked a crumb – of me.

Knowing God brings a hope that goes beyond the happiness we can experience in the world: joy deeper than fleeting happiness that is dependent upon others or on how our life's journey is going.

 Reflect

Spend some time quietly reflecting on where you might see hope, signs of renewal or a fresh start.

Even the tiniest, fragile hope can help us through a difficult season. Ask God to reveal hope to you anew if you are facing struggles or bring to mind those known to you who may be in need of hope.

 Pray

Source of all hope, robins remind us that even in deepest winter we can sing. Let me look with hope for the spring to come. In every season, may I know the promise of times yet to come and praise you in the place I find myself now. Amen.

15

Shaping our hearts

> '**I** will give you a new heart and put a new spirit in you; I will remove from you your heart of stone and give you a heart of flesh.'
> EZEKIEL 36:26

In the delightful book *What Katy Did* by Susan Coolidge, I was introduced to the determined character Katy Carr, living in a fictional Ohio town in the 1860s. Decades since reading this book, I have never forgotten one of Katy's realisations about how to approach people we find hard to connect with. She is encouraged to imagine that each person we encounter has two 'handles', a smooth one and a rough one. The key is to discover the smooth one. This might be praying for a way to unlock conversation, perhaps discovering their favourite hobby or talking about their beloved pet. I have often sought wisdom to find the smooth handle with someone who is hard to get alongside. The key is sometimes held in understanding what has caused someone's rough edges.

We can all develop a toughened exterior, made jagged by life experiences. Yet just like Katy determining to find that smooth handle, God longs to smooth our stubborn, roughly hewn hearts. We are all shaped by the hard times we go through, but God sees our smooth handle and wants to change and mould us.

Like the pebbles we find on a beach that have been transformed into tactile shapes by going through rough waters, our hearts can be made smooth by the loving hand of God. Among pebbles of varying shapes and textures, we can sometimes find one that has been shaped into a heart. These stones changed as they passed through rocks and rushing rivers. Smoothed gradually by all they go through, they eventually become the beautiful heart shape that so captivates those who collect these reminders in nature of love. These stones smoothed by the waters are no longer the shape they were, just as our hearts can be refined, transformed and healed over time.

Times of grief, joy and waiting all shape who we are. God has the power to transform hearts when someone encounters him and opens their heart to his redeeming power. This can be a 'road to Damascus' moment for some, a full 180-degree turn in their lives; but it can also be the gentle refining work of many seasons, even a lifetime, continuing to submit to God's almighty transformation.

It may be that you are praying for someone to have their heart changed or you feel there is part of your own heart that still needs smoothing. Rendering our hearts to God on our journey of faith allows him to gradually smooth out our jagged parts.

Reflect

Ask God to smooth away any rough edges in you, reflecting on how he has smoothed out your heart in the past.

Consider those people or situations where you need to find the smooth 'handle', asking God for wisdom to discern this when all you can see is the rough edges.

Pray

Lord God, remove any sharp edges I have yet to let you smooth. Refine and mould me daily. May I find the smooth 'handle' in the situations I face or with people I find difficult to understand. Amen.

16

Stargazing

> When I consider your heavens, the work of your fingers, the moon and the stars, which you have set in place, what is mankind that you are mindful of them, human beings that you care for them?
> PSALM 8:3–4

In the countryside of Normandy, we saw an incredibly clear sky at night. Stars seemed so much brighter against the deep ink black expanse that spread above, unblemished by light pollution. Constellations were visible and even shooting stars were seen darting across the night sky.

We often need to take a few moments to adjust our eyes to see stars, looking up, away from the distractions in the world around us. As we focus, we see pinpricks of light breaking through. The more we look, the more we see the stars that shine in even the darkest night. They are almost invisible at first, yet we begin to see them, the wonder of creation displayed. When light feels overcome by darkness, barely visible, may we have the strength to pause and look more carefully to see the light.

Psalm 147 reminds us that the God who orchestrates the stars can bring healing to our hurts: 'He heals the broken-hearted and binds up their wounds. He determines the number of the stars and calls them each by name' (vv. 3–4). Elisabeth Elliot (1926–2015), a Christian missionary, author and speaker who knew much personal tragedy, reflected on these reassuring, awe-inspiring verses of scripture, saying: 'If you are broken-hearted today, remember it's the same one who numbers the stars and calls them by name who can heal your heart.'

Stars appear to twinkle (scintillate) because their light bounces off different layers of the earth's atmosphere and changes direction. They appear tiny and distant to our earth-dwelling eyes, yet some stars are bigger and brighter than our sun!

The same God who set the stars in their paths – who knows each star that burns out and who called into being galaxies that stretch farther than the human mind or science can even comprehend – meets us in the place of grief, loss, pain and disappointment. In our darkest hour, when the darkness around seems all-consuming, light can break through. The hands that put the stars into space were pierced for our transgressions, surrendered to death so that we might know light and life in all its fullness.

Take time to look for long enough to see all the beauty and light that God has for you. Adjust your vision and pause to look up and see God at work, even in the times of darkness.

Reflect

Reflect on times that God helped you overcome darkness to see his light shining through circumstances, and give thanks.

Pause to consider that the maker of heaven and earth, whose hands flung stars into space, longs to hold you close and lift you up.

Pray

Father of the stars, may I see the light that shines in even the darkest skies. Remind me to look up, away from the distractions and artificial lights that dazzle, pausing long enough to see each light in the heavens. I pray for breakthrough in your name, light piercing the darkest of oppression. Amen.

17

Swans a-swimming

> Do nothing out of selfish ambition or vain conceit. Rather, in humility value others above yourselves, not looking to your own interests but each of you to the interests of the others.
> PHILIPPIANS 2:3–4

A swan gently glides across a still pond or down a river; it appears so serene and calming to observe. Almost regal in their bearing, the seemingly effortless action of a swan hides beneath it the powerful movement of their legs to propel them onwards. Perhaps this might remind us to consider people around us. We do not always know the struggles that others are going through, the battles they hide from the world. That person who always seems to have it all together may look to the outside observer as if they are gliding along with everything fine and calm. Yet so often, behind the serenity we see, people are carrying burdens of worry or illness, fighting battles that we simply have no idea they are dealing with.

Swans feature in the traditional carol 'The Twelve Days of Christmas'. The history of this well-known song has many versions. The Celtic explanation of the 'swans a-swimming' links them to the movements of the seven planets known at the time, but in the 17th century, when the carol is thought to date from, the swan was viewed as a good omen, being good to eat and a source of feathers and down – a generous gift for someone's true love to give! Some commentaries believe that the 'seven swans a-swimming' represent the seven gifts of the Holy Spirit, mentioned in Romans 12:6–8. These are prophecy, serving, teaching, encouraging, giving, leadership and showing mercy, and they are seen as important in our spiritual growth.

We all wear masks at times. Even the most poised and confident person we meet could be dealing with an inner turmoil, a well of uncertainty or need, hiding behind what we see. Perhaps you are putting on a brave face or a calm exterior to not worry or involve other people. Self-doubt, worry and insecurities are not always written on our face and can be hidden behind layers of self-protection and a well-practised appearance of calmness and control. Yet when we share our struggles, we can find a lightness and a way forward, with others helping to lift our burdens, knowing we no longer need to hide behind a facade.

 Reflect

Could it be that you need to take off your swan-like facade, be honest and real with someone and ask for help?

Might there be someone around you who needs to unburden themselves? Ask God to give you eyes to see those in need, those who may not be as okay as they appear.

Pray

Gracious God, you see behind the mask I show to the world. Give me the courage to ask for support when I am struggling to stay afloat. Show me where I can gently draw alongside others, that they might be able to share honestly about the battles they are facing, knowing it's okay to not have it all together. Amen.

18

Evergreen love

> Give thanks to the Lord, for he is good; his love endures forever.
> PSALM 107:1

When we think of Christmas, we often picture those traditional evergreen trees, covered in numerous fairy lights. Decorating our Christmas tree each year is one of my favourite activities, as we prepare our home and our hearts to celebrate Christmas. I delight in the annual unpacking of our precious collection of ornaments, accumulated over the years. They are memories wrapped up in tissue and rediscovered each year, reminders of places visited, gifts from loved ones and the new additions each year that our children make. I even have a treasured red apple ornament, which hung on the 1980s white tinsel tree when I was growing up.

The tradition of decorating a Christmas tree is thought to have begun in Germany, with 16th-century records showing that devout Christians displayed decorated trees in their homes. In 1846, Queen Victoria and her German Prince, Albert, appeared in *The Illustrated London News* in a sketch of the royal family, standing around a Christmas tree. This innovation by the popular royals was swiftly adopted by their admiring subjects. Many believe that Martin Luther, the 16th-century Protestant reformer, was the first to add tree lights in the form of candles, inspired by the sight of stars above one winter night.

For Christians, the adorning of evergreen branches reflects the promise of everlasting life with Jesus, and the constancy of God that does not falter or fade with the turn of the seasons. We can be confident in the knowledge that whatever we do, there is nothing that can lessen or lose the unchanging love of God. God's love does not grow weary, diminish or fall away with the seasons. His love and mercy are as strong and vibrant today as they were the moment you first encountered them.

God remains faithful for all eternity. There is no greater love or constant we can know in our lives. However much we might doubt, struggle or slip away, God is still watching over us. His love is yours forever and nothing will ever change that. Take a moment to let that truth sink in. What incredible, amazing grace!

The sight of unwavering greenery in the seemingly lifeless months of winter, when nature is in hibernation, reminds us of the love that God lavishes on us, all year round. The enduring love of God is evergreen, a lasting kindness and consistency that doesn't fade or die with the season or the vacillating seasons of our hearts. It is forever faithful and unfading, like evergreen trees.

Reflect

Spend some time in quiet reflection, giving thanks to God for his eternal love and constancy in every season.

Consider those who have been your evergreens: people who have remained constant in the journey of your life and weathered the winters of life with you, remaining when other friendships and relationships have faded and gone. Thank God for them.

Pray

Constant God, your love does not fade or alter with the changing seasons of our life. You are faithful, no matter what we face. Help me to turn to you afresh and accept your love that lasts forever. I am grateful for those who have faithfully journeyed with me in every season. I give you thanks for them. Amen.

19

Working in the waiting

> Now faith is confidence in what we hope for and assurance about what we do not see.
> HEBREWS 11:1

In the dark months of winter, there is much unseen growth going on. Germination, preparation and slow progress are happening, so plants, flowers and trees can spring forth with new life in the coming seasons. Yet this cannot be rushed. If it happened too rapidly, a tender, growing sapling, bud or shoot would perish in the frosts of winter. With the right amount of time to grow below the ground or in the bare branches of a tree, new life awaits, ready to emerge in the warm sunshine of spring.

In the same way, God is working in the waiting when we feel lost in the wilderness or progress is halted, readying us for the next season. Desolate places can be preparing the ground; a season of learning through hardship, frustration and seeming inertia. Accepting, even embracing times of waiting can be hard, with our human impatience, but this space often brings forth new revelation. Unplanned pauses can be God preparing us for the seasons yet to come.

God is always on the move, yet this can be small unseen victories, life-changing moments disguised as gentle steps forward. Work that goes on beneath the soil before we see growth is significant. We often try to rush the time of fruition, perhaps in our prayers or personal life, wanting to achieve a certain goal or impatient to see others come to faith. Yet we trust in the unseen God and can cling to hope, even when our prayers seem to go unanswered.

In the depths of winter all appears still, hibernating or even dead – yet spring always comes. Our creator God is always working for our good, even when situations feel hopeless or stalled entirely. There is work to be done in the waiting, as God prepares the ground of our lives, nurturing and sustaining us in the seasons of seeming inaction.

When the first green shoots break through the seemingly barren winter soil, much growth has already gone on. Being sure of what we hope for might mean believing for a brighter day when all seems dark or trusting for an end to a difficult situation or for healing or restoration of a relationship. We hope in the yet to come. Being confident in a future that we can't yet see is possible because we trust in the visible moving of our unseen God.

Reflect

Seeds and bulbs are not buried but planted; they are put in the soil to grow not to die. Give thanks for the new beginnings God has provided, or pray for patience in a season of waiting.

Life is present in even the tiniest seed. So much potential held in something small. Reflect on something that seems like it isn't growing in your life, and ask God to renew your hope in the unseen work he is doing.

Pray

Unseen God, thank you that I can know that you are working in the seasons of waiting. You are working, even when my eyes do not see, just as so many things go on in nature all around us, unnoticed. Thank you, Lord, that you are never dormant, that hope springs eternal and it will flourish at just the right time. Amen.

20

Spring is coming

> 'See, I am doing a new thing! Now it springs up; do you not perceive it? I am making a way in the wilderness and streams in the wasteland.'
> ISAIAH 43:19

Winter may linger, as we yearn for the coming of spring. Yet without fail the seasons turn. Life begins to spring forth. In her poignant verses entitled 'Awakening', American Christian poet Margaret Elizabeth Sangster (1838–1912) reflects on this, rejoicing that: 'Never yet was a springtime, late though lingered the snow, that the sap stirred not at the whisper, of the south wind, sweet and low.' The poet's works are characterised by themes of nature and faith, hope and renewal.

There is something defiantly hopeful about watching spring unfold. God's power is reassuringly reflected in the unrelenting march of nature. Nature springs forth undeterred in its ordained season. Bulbs and trees sprout once more with the green of new life, from the seemingly dead soil and bare branches of winter. The promise of Genesis 8:22 remains: 'As long as the earth endures, seedtime and harvest, cold and heat, summer and winter, day and night will never cease.' We can know new life and a fresh hope, that springs eternal.

How often, though, do we only notice flowers once they are in full bloom, missing the less obvious signs of new growth as they quietly break through the soil? We can become too caught up in daily life to stop long enough to see tiny shoots appearing, missing the growth stage. Change and progress in life can so easily be dismissed or missed. As we impatiently hurry to see the blossoming, we miss the buds.

One of the first signs that spring is on the way, often easily missed, is the emergence of snowdrops. It is always a surprise when I discover these determined little flowers among the frosty ground. Before the coming of springtime, they begin to appear, often far earlier than most flowers, heralding longer, sunnier days.

In the Victorian language of flowers, snowdrops symbolise hope and consolation. Known also as Candlemas bells since the Middle Ages, when they were used to decorate churches, snowdrops represent new beginnings, rebirth and the ability to overcome challenges. Historically, these hardy little flowers, which appear so delicate, were thought to ease headaches. In modern medicine a compound from the bulb, called galantamine, has been used to treat Alzheimer's disease. Incredibly, snowdrops contain a natural antifreeze, which allows them to survive the frosty nights and recover once temperatures in the day begin to rise. Because of this, snowdrop bulbs were utilised during World War I to de-ice tanks!

God's Spirit at work in us can provide a strength that goes beyond our human capacity, an inner 'antifreeze' like that of the snowdrops, helping us to withstand the harsh seasons and cling to an everlasting hope. Keep looking for signs of renewal and hope, in even the hardest times, trusting that circumstances will change, new beginnings are possible. Hold on, spring is coming.

 Reflect

What signs of new growth or moving forward are you waiting for that you could miss if you're not watching carefully? Think of those green shoots on trees, which can often be missed until the full flowers or leaves have bloomed.

Remember spring is coming. Keep looking for breakthrough. It may be small steps forward, like tiny shoots of hope bursting forth.

Pray

Unseen one, I can be impatient for change, wanting to rush ahead to the next season. Yet I know that you are working in the waiting, preparing me for what is to come. Help me to trust you are not dormant and to look for signs of new life springing forth, not missing the signs of progress, trusting your perfect timing. Amen.

Spring

# 21

Hidden beauty

> Let us not become weary in doing good, for at the proper time we will reap a harvest if we do not give up.
> GALATIANS 6:9

There is such a wonderful curiosity when moving into a new home, not knowing what flowers might bloom in the garden or in local parks and grass verges, as each season unfolds. I remember the delightful surprise upon seeing the colourful array of crocuses, which unexpectedly broke through the green expanse of lawn in front of our new home, in springtime. We had no idea that the vibrant crocuses were quietly waiting, unseen, beneath the surface of the grass, preparing to duly appear when the spring sunshine warmed the earth and winter had passed.

Like vibrant paint speckled across the blank canvas of the lawn, dear little perennial crocuses appeared annually without fail after that. Just as they had likely done for countless years before that and in the years since life has moved us on. It was, of course, less unexpected in subsequent years after we first beheld these tiny flowers, yet it remained just as uplifting a sight with each coming spring.

Flowers appear, sprouting through the surface of the soil, at just the right time for them to flourish. Much of the growth needed by a crocus, like other bulbs or seeds, goes on unseen below the surface. These beautiful, colourful plants that suddenly seem to be painted upon the grass in springtime bloom only when the conditions are exactly right. Timing is everything. If flowers, fruit or crops were to grow too early they would perish, unprepared and unequipped to survive the much colder seasons.

How reassuring are the words from Ecclesiastes 3:11 that tell how our creator God 'has made everything beautiful in its time'. We often seek to rush to the next stage, impatient to see the fruition of seeds of faith we plant or to complete a goal or see a dream realised. This heartening verse reminds us that God has a plan. Everything springs forth at the appointed time, each plant flourishes in its correct season and at the right moment within that season, not before. We also grow in our faith at the time and pace that is right for us on our individual journey with God, who ordered the seasons into being.

 Reflect

In what areas of your life might you need to remember that the time to see growth or fruition may require patience?

Think back to times in the past when you saw growth when it seemed that there would be none. Give thanks for these and be encouraged that God brings about all things, in their season.

Consider any current frustrations in your work, family or ministry life where it seems that nothing is flourishing, and place these in God's hands.

Pray

Lord, there is such a wonder of hidden beauty in creation. May I trust that you are always working, below the surface of what is seen, to bring situations to light at the appointed time. I can rely on your consistency, testifying from seasons past and trusting for the times ahead. Forgive my human impatience and remind me that you make everything beautiful in the right timing and not before. Amen.

22

Busy bees

> '*Come to me, all you who are weary and burdened, and I will give you rest. Take my yoke upon you and learn from me, for I am gentle and humble in heart, and you will find rest for your souls.*'
> MATTHEW 11:28–29

In the garden, I watched as bees buzzed busily around the flowers in the sunshine. It was an unexpected day of enforced rest, due to straining my back, that gave me time to just simply sit and observe the sights, sounds and fragrances of the glorious nature around me. I began to wonder if the bees appreciate the beauty of each flower or if they focus purely on the important task of pollen gathering. Can they even comprehend the splendour of a flower or are they only attracted to the bright colours and fragrant perfume it exudes because of the nectar within?

Scientific research into the behaviour of bees observes that they are drawn to the fragrance of flowers and are especially attracted to blue, purple and yellow petals.

Scientists have also discovered that flowers have ultraviolet patterns on their petals that guide the bees to the pollen but are invisible to the human eye!

Being busy is celebrated in modern society and often, when we take a pause, it is viewed by others or ourselves as laziness. We equate rest with a lack of productivity and wasting time. Yet God calls us to find rest in him, to take refuge in him when we are weary, to lay our labours down and simply come to him. How often we 'buzz' around continually and forget to trust our burdens into his care.

Sometimes we need to stop buzzing around and pause, to appreciate the beauty around us and find refreshment through time with God. We can be so occupied with work, family life or in our ministry, our days so full, that we miss the blessings and beauty of the moment or even burn out entirely. Taking time to simply pause, breathe, reflect and appreciate the work God is doing through us and around us – stopping to 'smell the roses' – is never a waste of time.

Rest is so important, enabling us to refocus and renew our strength. Jesus rested, spending time in quiet contemplation, waiting upon God. He understood the need to withdraw, to take time to find a place of solitude and rest as he faced the work ahead, to fulfil God's plan.

Reflect

What burdens do you need to give over to God?

How might you find space to pause and rest, to appreciate the beauty around you, among the busyness of life?

Pray

Lord, help me to find rest in you. May I take time to pause and draw near to you. Help me to see the beauty in the moment and feel renewed. Amen.

23

Nesting season

> You hem me in behind and before, and you lay your hand upon me.
> PSALM 139:5

Waking to the sounds of a huge storm, I became aware of this forecasted meteorological onslaught, that we had not realised would hit our locality with the force that it did. The day progressed with increasing reports of its impact nationally and local news of the tearing down of older, less firmly rooted trees and a devastation of floored fence panels. Road closures were put in place for several days after, as work began to remove felled trees that were making many roads temporarily impassable. Other areas of the country experienced more long-lasting impacts with homes flooded and other damage done.

I recalled again, as I listened to the storm that continued to rattle the windows throughout the day, glad to be safely at home, a story my mum told me as a child. She would tell me, as I settled into bed on a stormy night, to imagine I was a baby bird, cosy in their nest. Fledglings rest secure in the protection and comfort of the nest, built by the parent birds to provide a place of safety from the storms that might surround them. Even now when I hear heavy rainfall or high winds, as I settle at night I think of this comforting image of being sheltered from the elements and have shared this with my own children, on blustery or stormy nights, as I tucked them into their 'nest'.

The phrase 'You hem me in', used in Psalm 139, suggests a sense of divine protection, tightly sewn around on every side. The Hebrew root word used here is *tsur*, meaning to enclose or bind and which speaks of God's presence encompassing us. The idea is that the Lord is securing us on all sides, not to prevent our freedom but encircling us with protection, a guiding hand like a shepherd enclosing his flock to keep them safe from harm.

Comfort not restriction: we can be held safe in the arms of God daily. The knowledge of God's protection and presence in every storm that rages means we can know a sensation of warmth and care. Like a tiny bird or egg, safe and secure in the carefully constructed nest, sheltered beneath the feathers of its parent as they grow. Fledglings are watched over, fed and nurtured, their every need met, until the time is right for them to take that first, tentative flight and leave the nest.

 Reflect

Might you need to simply ask God to hem you in? To know the comfort of his embrace, secure and safe in his arms?

Perhaps take some time to close your eyes, asking God to encircle you afresh with his loving care.

Pray

Father God, thank you that you hem me in. You surround and hold me, no matter what storm buffets me. I can know security and safety in your everlasting arms. Amen.

24

A carpet of bluebells

> There is a time for everything, and a season for every activity under the heavens: a time to be born and a time to die, a time to plant and a time to uproot.
> ECCLESIASTES 3:1–2

I had seen many beautiful photographs springing up on my social media feed, yet each year I had missed the chance to see local woodlands carpeted in bluebells by the time I was aware that they had bloomed. Imagine my joy when we met with friends at a local heritage site on a sunny April day to be greeted by the warmly welcoming staff member who exclaimed that this was the very best weekend to see their bluebell wood! We had not gone with the intention of seeing the bluebells that day, but we were able to wander among the trees, where it seemed like the entire floor of their little woodlands was covered with these sweet little flowers.

Within a matter of days or weeks at most, though, these bluebells would have started to fade away. Bluebells are so brief in their season, one of the last spring flowers to bloom before the woodland canopy is created by new leaves that block out the sunlight. It is sad, when they bloom with such vitality, that their time in the sun is so short. But the bluebells remained in my memory, captured in photos I took, and they brought such joy.

We can sometimes feel that the impact we have made in our life or ministry has had little effect. Perhaps our time in a role or place was cut short or was not the season we had anticipated. But just as the bluebells created an unforgettable memory, we can trust that God can do great things through us, even in a brief season. Never underestimate the impact you can make in the briefest of conversations or times with those you meet in your ministry, work or family life.

Seeds of faith and kingdom work can be planted even in a short space of time; in a moment's encounter God can move and change lives. When life moves us on, the impact we have made in a fleeting time can have eternal significance, just as the joy felt upon beholding a carpet of bluebells can last far beyond the time they flourish, their beauty living on in photos and our memories.

May you know that you have been a bluebell in someone else's life.

 Reflect

Reflect on a time that was brief and perhaps painful in its ending but had a huge impact or significance in your life or faith journey.

Bring to God any feelings of upset, bitterness or regret, asking that he might help you to see what growth there was in that short season.

Give thanks for those people, situations or relationships that have been like bluebells in your life. With you for a short time, yet their impact lasts a lifetime.

Pray

God of mercy, lead me to a place of relinquishing my bitterness, seeking instead to trust that seeds of faith – the impact made, however small it may have felt – can have eternal consequences. Remind me of those who have been the bluebells in my life's path. I give thanks for them. Amen.

25

In the valley

> You who abide in the shelter of the Most High, who rest in the shadow of the Almighty, say to the Lord, 'You are my refuge and my fortress, my God in whom I place my trust.'
> PSALM 91:1–2 (NCB)

Some plants can only thrive in the shadows of a valley, sheltered and protected from the elements. Lily of the valley flowers grow in the shade, their flowers bending over beneath the cover of their wide, green leaves. They have biblical links, described as an emblem of humility, reflecting the character of the Lord Jesus Christ, who was bowed low upon the cross. The lily of the valley is also referred to as Mary's tears, referencing a biblical connection with Mary weeping at Jesus' crucifixion, and it is also fabled to have first bloomed where Eve's tears fell as she left the garden of Eden.

There are times in life when we are soaring, reaching new heights. We can also go through seasons when we hit a low point, perhaps a time of ill health, worry or struggles. It is often amid these rock-bottom experiences that we need God most. When we reflect, with hindsight, we see that some of our most significant growth happened during the 'valley' days.

Growth can't always happen when we are on the mountaintops of life. It is here where we are vulnerable, like plants that perish in the open, with no shelter from the sun or wind. Valleys can provide much-needed protection. There are times when we need to take refuge, safe from harm. Grounded yet sheltered, in the shadow of the Almighty. God often uses the 'valley' days to nourish us, preparing and strengthening us for the next season.

 Reflect

How might God be using your current season to prepare you for the days to come?

Reflect on times when God used the 'valley' days to help you develop, safe in his protection.

Pray

Lord, thank you that you are my strength when I soar, but that you also shelter me and are my refuge. Protector God, help me to know that when I go through the valley, you are with me, and to trust you to enable me to grow and thrive in each season. Amen.

26

Like the weather

> Every good and perfect gift is from above, coming down from the Father of the heavenly lights, who does not change like shifting shadows.
> JAMES 1:17

I sat writing the first draft of this reflection on a day when there had been hail in April but also bursts of glorious sunshine. A timely example of the changeable weather of spring, hail had suddenly bounced noisily off car bonnets outside, only to stop moments later and be replaced by a sky of clear blue, sunshine glinting off the car paintwork that had so unexpectedly been hit by hailstones.

Blue skies and sunshine can feel at odds with the rain, hail or even snow showers. It is as though there is a battle waging between spring and winter, with the appearance of warm spells and sunshine, yet frosty mornings and winter rain are reluctant to retreat. It is not an exaggeration to say that the weather during April, in England, can feel like we experience all four seasons in one day. The weather is slowly changing, improving but not yet fully transformed into the new season we long for, after the cold and dark of winter.

Beauty can come out of our fiercest battles. Like a rainbow following a storm, we see the promise held for so long come to fruition or something happening that we didn't imagine was possible. Without this combination of weather conditions, we would not see the most incredible arching rainbows, a symbol of hope over adversity, fresh starts in times of despondency and a reminder that God is faithful. We see within the changeable weather of spring a glimpse of the summer yet to come.

There are times when the behaviour of other people and, if we are honest, our own moods, can change from moment to moment – disappointment to joy and back again, upset replaced with delight. Emotions are as changeable as the weather, and they often take us by surprise or leave us reeling, like a sudden rain shower in April, over just as quickly as it began. Life can bring a rollercoaster of experiences – it is not all rainbows and sunshine, yet each day holds hope. Light can still be seen, though it may only be slowly breaking through.

God does not always stop the rains that fall. We can hold firm to the knowledge that he is with us in all weathers. Bearing us up in the deluge, whispering in the storm, 'I am with you.' It can be hard to praise during storms, but we can trust that we will see the rainbow moments at last. Times of trials and testing may seem to hold sway, but we can look for rainbows; seasons will change and God is faithful.

 Reflect

Bring to God those things that feel uncertain. Know that sometimes you can only go a moment or day at a time, but the skies will clear and hope remains in every changing season.

Let go of hurt from those who change like the weather. Hold on to the faithfulness of God when your heart is troubled, when you go through deep waters or people do not remain faithful or dependable.

Pray

Unchanging one, rain will fall and clouds will come, but the sun will appear once more. Phases pass, trials do not last forever, and you are constant in every moment. Help me to look for the rainbow and hold on. Storms will pass away. Amen.

27

Where my help comes from

> I lift up my eyes to the mountains – where does my help come from? My help comes from the Lord, the Maker of heaven and earth.
> PSALM 121:1–2

These comforting verses taken from Psalm 121 were one of my Grandpa and Nanny's most beloved scriptures, and were inscribed in the Bible they gave me for my 18th birthday. The psalm holds a special place in my heart, and it has always felt especially poignant to read it when holidaying in my 'happy place', the Lake District. Though this area is named in recognition of the many expanses of water, it has picturesque panoramas of hills, providing a stunning backdrop to every view. Magnificent hills, which have inspired numerous poets and painters, invoke in me a deep sense of peace when travelling north from the Midlands. I still feel a pervading calm descend as the hills ascend higher, the motorway giving way to layers of fields and hills, striking in the colours of every season.

When I reread this psalm, preparing this reflection, I considered the meaning in the description of it as 'a song of ascent'. At first glance I misread this as 'assent', signifying an expression of approval or agreement. The actual word 'ascent' relates to the act of climbing, moving upward on a slope or pathway. This tells us of the context in which David wrote this psalm, as it is thought that in these verses he is contemplating the treacherous travel through the hills, looking to God, his source of strength. Perhaps God had prompted me to mistake the word, to ponder that in lifting our eyes to the Lord, who is with us on the 'ascents' of life, this also requires us to 'assent' to his leading. We are to trust the mountains we face into his care and ourselves to his divine protection.

When the road ahead is daunting, we can look beyond the limitations of the earthly realm, putting our confidence in God, the mountain maker and mover. Psalm 121 is part of a group of psalms thought to be sung by the people as they travelled to Jerusalem, with the 'ascent' referred to being the climb to reach the summit of Mount Moriah. These psalms were an expression of hope and belief in God's mercy and protection on the people's pilgrimage of faith.

Reaching high into the sky above the landscape below, hills and mountains can make us feel so small and insignificant compared to their lofty grandeur. Yet the creator who formed the earth cares about each one of us. The Lord of all creation can help us overcome the most mammoth of difficulties.

God, who made the mountains, so awe-inspiring in their heights, is also our refuge and fortress – our help in times of need. In lifting our eyes to the hills or mountains, we not only cast our gaze heavenward, to the God who formed the mountains that surround us, but we also look up from the cares or struggles we are facing on earth to cry out to the creator of heaven and earth.

 Reflect

God knows the mountains you are facing, the challenges that feel insurmountable and the rocky terrain you need to navigate. He is your source of strength and protection in the journey ahead.

Take some time to read the whole of Psalm 121, considering each verse and how it resonates with you. You might want to read it aloud, declaring your prayer of 'assent' to God.

 Pray

Elevated one, your majesty reigns above the earth, yet you care about each of us. Protection and deliverance are found in you, the source of my strength. Help me to remember that you are bigger than any mountain I face. You go with me and will not let me stumble or fall. Amen.

28

Flowing waters

> The wellspring of wisdom *is* a flowing brook.
> PROVERBS 18:4 (NKJV)

There is something so calming about water, yet it can also refresh and invigorate. I have always felt serene and close to God when I am in or near water, whether it be the tranquillity of floating in a millpond-like swimming pool, the saltwater buoyancy of the sea or being close to a crashing waterfall or a gentle, babbling brook.

Such wonder and awe are felt when hearing a rushing river or being near a waterfall. Think of the invigorating sight of rolling waves or the gentle melodic trickle of a shallow beck, rippling across colourful pebbles. Being near the running water of rivers, waterfalls or the sea can bring a sense of calm refreshment, and there is a reason for this. Tiny particles of negative ions are created by the movement of water in waterfalls, oceans and streams. These cannot be seen by the naked eye but carry a negative electrical charge that has a range of health benefits. Scientific research shows that they increase serotonin levels in the brain. Serotonin is a neurotransmitter vital in regulating mood, helping to alleviate depression, anxiety and stress. It has also been proven to reduce inflammation, enhance immune function and ease symptoms of asthma and insomnia.

Water is a source of vitality to all living things. Great power is displayed in a rushing river or the thundering deluge of waterfalls, but it can also be a soothing sound. A reminder that God is the provider of living water, our source of refreshment, the wellspring of our salvation. In the lyrics to the hymn 'My worth is not in what I own', Graham Kendrick declares the assurance of knowing God, our redeemer and 'wellspring of my soul'.

A wellspring is a fountain or spring that provides a constant supply of water. Describing God as the wellspring of our soul is to declare he is our supply, the water of life and unending source of our strength. This verse from Proverbs invites believers to rejoice in the assurance of God's salvation, to draw afresh from the wellspring of our salvation.

Unlike the renewing power of water that rejuvenates us for a time, God is the living water that never runs dry, the fountain ever flowing with the life-spring of strength. He is the source of all we need to sustain and refresh our being; quenching the thirsts no other water can: life bringing and revitalising.

 ## Reflect

Take some time to close your eyes and invite God to pour into those areas that need revitalising. Or simply ask him to be the wellspring of your soul, the source of your strength.

Where in your community or family are you praying for a wellspring of living water? Bring these before God, trusting that he can supply every need, bringing life in barren lands.

 ## Pray

Wellspring of my soul, you refresh and renew me daily with the river of mercy that never runs dry. Be my supply, the source of my vitality. Sustain me, even when the river runs dry, and help me to know refreshment and reinvigoration. Amen.

29

Beneath his wings

> He will cover you with his feathers, and under his wings you will find refuge; his faithfulness will be your shield and rampart.
> PSALM 91:4

When they were smaller, our boys delighted in spotting interesting feathers in the park or on a pavement. These unexpected treasures gave them great joy, akin to that felt when they found a particularly pleasing stick or pebble along our path. There were times when we had to gently convince them to not bring home every rain- and mud-soaked feather or chunk of rock that we found out and about, though we were happy to see their wonder in the natural world. They are older now, but are still captivated by interesting river rocks, shells or pebbles on a beach. I hope they never lose this joy in God's creation and the incredible nature we walk among.

In the Bible, feathers and birds are symbolic of divine protection, reminding us of God's constant presence in our lives and his provision for all he has made. Even in the storms of life, we can know shelter beneath the wings of the Almighty. Powerful, yet gentle when we draw near to him, God can keep us in perfect peace, whatever life may bring.

Deceptive in their lightness and soft texture, feathers are designed to provide birds with protection against the unforgiving elements. Birds are the only animals that have feathers, giving a unique defence from injury, waterproofing and insulation from both cold and heat, as seasons change. Feathers are arranged in symmetrical tracts known as 'pterylae', and are made of keratin, the same lightweight material as our hair and fingernails. Soft downy feathers trap pockets of air close to the body, to keep birds warm, and birds fluff their feathers when it is cold to trap more air, allowing them to stay warmer.

Feathers carry a range of symbolism and hold significance to many. Some believe they are a sign that a departed loved one or angels are watching over you and that God is listening to our prayers. Feathers are linked to hope, rebirth and renewal, just as birds shed and regrow their feathers.

The assurance that the Lord is our refuge is described with beautiful imagery in Psalm 91, with the invitation to shelter beneath his wings, covered with the protection of his love. Under God's wings is our shelter in the storm, where we can rest safely. To be covered in this way is not only comforting, but also the ultimate peace, placing ourselves into the comfort of God's arms, to dwell in his protection.

Reflect

Do you need to simply rest today, safe under his wings, accepting the protection and care of the everlasting God?

Reflect on the promise of Psalm 91 and the words of Psalm 32:7: 'You are my hiding-place; you will protect me from trouble and surround me with songs of deliverance.' Declare this truth over any troubles you are facing or those of others God has laid on your heart.

Pray

My refuge, thank you for your protection in times of trouble. Help me to remember that you are my hiding place; I can find shelter beneath your wings. Amen.

30

Fragrant rain

> Let my teaching fall like rain and my words descend like dew, like showers on new grass, like abundant rain on tender plants.
> DEUTERONOMY 32:2

Nature awakens the senses to wonder and awe. Sights, sounds and scents that can evoke strong remembrances and bring refreshment to the soul. The invigorating smell of the salty sea before you even see it, the shimmer of sunlight on the ocean or a cry from seagulls overhead in the city can transport us to the seaside holidays of childhood. Memories long forgotten are brought into sharp focus by the aroma of familiar food or the faintest detection of a perfume, transporting us to a point in time or recalling a particular person or event.

The smell of trees and grass after rainfall evokes in me a sense of peace, the scent of nature awakened. David Takayoshi Suzuki, Canadian academic, science broadcaster and environmental activist, said of the power nature has to inspire the senses:

> Feel the rain and wind on your face, smell the fragrance of soil and ocean, gaze at the spectacle of the myriad stars in clear air… Doing so will rekindle that sense of wonder and excitement we all had as children discovering the world and will engender a feeling of peace and harmony at being in balance with the natural world that is our home.

In 2 Corinthians, Paul uses the example of a Roman victory parade, where a triumphant general would be led with his captives through the streets and the sweet scent of incense would fill the air. Paul gives thanks that God 'uses us to spread the aroma of the knowledge of him everywhere' (2:14), exclaiming one verse later: 'For we are to God the pleasing aroma of Christ among those who are being saved and those who are perishing.' This can seem like a daunting task to undertake, yet we are simply called to make God known: to live our lives as a fragrant offering to God and to bear witness to the relationship we have with him. We are to take this 'fragrance' out into the world, that others might know the good news of Jesus, like the unmistakable scent of the sweet incense that burned in the tabernacle, signifying the presence of God.

 Reflect

Consider the scents that evoke memories for you. You might want to step outside or plan time to take a walk and allow the scents of nature to awaken your senses or give you a fresh moment of tranquillity.

What memory might God bring to your mind through familiar fragrances? Perhaps a happy memory or significant moment in your life or in your walk with God?

 Pray

Creator God, awaken my senses. Help me to pause and experience the fragrances of nature, so vital and refreshing. Help me to spread the 'fragrance' of your presence in my life, that others may know the sweet aroma of Christ that brings life. Amen.

Summer

Psalm 139:17-18 How precious are your thoughts about me, O God

31

Grains of sand

> How precious are your thoughts about me, O God. They cannot be numbered! I can't even count them; they outnumber the grains of sand.
> PSALM 139:17–18 (NLT)

Have you ever held sand and then let it pour through your fingers? It is hard to imagine how many grains of sand cascade down from even a small handful, and even more unfathomable to consider how many are found on a beach or in the expanse of a desert – countless tiny grains of sand. It is incredible that the God who knows each grain of sand thinks of us.

David's marvelling praise in Psalm 139 exclaims that the thoughts the Lord has of him outnumber the grains of sand. It's hard to begin to comprehend how many that is. The sheer magnitude of grains of sand found on even the smallest beach is astounding. Research estimates that there are roughly 8 billion grains of sand per cubic metre, and roughly 700 billion cubic metres of sand on earth. That equates to approximately 5 sextillion grains in total – a phenomenal figure, beyond human comprehension.

The uniqueness and beauty contained within the minuscule form of sand is incredible to behold, seen in amazing microscope images. Photographs reveal individual facets created under pressure, over time made beautiful because of what they've been through. Sand is made of tiny pieces of weathered rock, broken down and eroded, over millions of years. It contains mineral pieces, bits of lava, coral and volcanic crystals. The reshaping that occurs along the way often begins thousands of miles from where it is found, compressed by rocks and ground down. The vastness of sand on the face of the earth is even more awe-inspiring when we consider that each individual grain contains its own arrangement of microscopic treasure.

In this psalm, David writes with awe about the God who knows each detail of our lives, the creator who has known us before we were even conceived. There is nowhere we can go that is outside of his care. How valuable then must we be in the sight of God! In the Middle Ages, Julian of Norwich, the anchoress and writer of the earliest surviving works in English by a woman, declared: 'For we are so preciously loved by God that we cannot even comprehend it.'

We can feel insignificant on earth, compared to the vastness of sand upon the land and below the seas, yet God considers you and thought you worth facing death itself, to bring you closer to him. You were created entirely individual, like each grain of sand, and the creator of the universe cares about the smallest detail of your life, your worries and your joys.

Reflect

Are you feeling ground down today? Bring before God the things that are compressing and wearing you down.

Are you aware of the unseen beauty within you – the things that make you precious in God's sight? Even if you find this hard to see or believe, know that the creator who made you knows and loves you.

Reflect on the awesome truth that God cares deeply about what you go through and give thanks for ways God has already shaped you and journeyed with you to where you are now.

Pray

Transforming God, it is easy to feel insignificant, when I consider the expanse of sand upon the earth, the galaxies above and the seas below. But you value each of us and see the beauty you created within each of us. Thank you, Lord, that your thoughts of me outnumber the grains of sand and you care for me. Amen.

32

Where we are planted

> So then, just as you received Christ Jesus as Lord, continue to live your lives in him, rooted and built up in him, strengthened in the faith as you were taught, and overflowing with thankfulness.
> COLOSSIANS 2:6–7

I remember being fascinated at the sight of the hydrangea plant, blooming with colour in the garden of a friend's house, which we passed on the school run. Growing right next to the pavement, I would often stop to take a closer look at this delightful cloud of vibrant and varied colours. Each hydrangea shrub appears in a slightly different hue to the next, with these shades determined by the type of soil in which they grow. Beautiful blends of colour can even be seen across the petals of a single flower, with variant shades of blue, purple or pink, like a wash of watercolour paint.

These intriguing flowers present different colours depending on the levels of acid or alkaline minerals present in the soil – a pH level of 5.5 or lower will produce blue flowers, 6.5 or higher will grow pink flowers, and anything in between 5.5 and 6.5 will create purple flowers. The colour shades across a plant can range from the palest of pinks, lavenders or powder blues, to deep shades of purple, red and royal blue. The coloration of these delicate petals also depends on the quantity of aluminium ions in the soil and the additives the plant takes in through its roots. Curiously, adding some everyday products to the soil can also influence this, including eggshells, which reduce the acidity of the soil, raising the pH level, to produce pinker blooms, or coffee grounds, which conversely lower the pH level, resulting in bluer shades developing.

Where we are planted, the environment we live in, can impact how we bloom. We can, to some extent, choose where we grow in a way a hydrangea cannot. We can make conscious decisions about what nourishes us and what we absorb, like how we spend our free time or who we share our lives with. The books or blogs we read, the podcasts or people we listen to and the content we consume through social media, films and television all influence us. However, we can often be impacted by our environment without even realising it.

The 'true colours' of a hydrangea flower reveal where it has been planted; what has fed it and helped it to grow is reflected in the appearance of the petals. Are we taking in the right nutrients that will help us to flourish? Do we need to come back to the source of our growth and strength, to be nourished afresh by God's word, his promises and the strength we draw from being rooted in the soil of his grace?

 Reflect

What additives are you allowing into the soil of your life? Is your being rooted in faith visible to others?

How might the things that you are taking in through your roots impact on your growth and the person you are?

Take some time to consider what you could add to your life to nourish and grow you in your faith. Be honest with yourself about what has a negative influence on your colours.

Pray

Loving Lord, may your word be my sustenance, my life showing that I am nourished by being planted in the rich soil of your grace. I pray that your love would be evident in me. Help me to bloom with the colours that reflect your greatness and the difference it makes being rooted in you. Amen.

33

Breaking waves

> You rule over the surging sea; when its waves mount up, you still them.
> PSALM 89:9

Standing on a beach in Dorset, watching the waves, I was awestruck by the expanse of the sea before me. The waves off Portland Bill collide with a shallow underwater ledge of rock jutting out into the sea. These treacherous tidal flows create huge waves that move in different directions, a rolling swell crashing without ceasing. Seeing these waters, seemingly unending as they stretched beyond the horizon, my soul bubbled up with worship, amazed and humbled by the vast majesty of nature. The exhilarating power on display can make us feel tiny and insignificant by comparison. We stand in awe of the might of the sea yet can trust in the constancy of the wave maker, the tide turner.

The magnificent rise and fall of the waves is a joy to behold when we are safe on the shore. Yet there is also a sense of necessary reverence and respect for the strength of the waves, the undercurrent that can easily drag someone down. We feel a heightened sense of human fragility compared to the power of the mighty ocean, with its dangerous potential.

There are times in life that feel overwhelming, like waves are crashing in from every direction, yet God who tells the waves to rise is ready to gently lift us above the swell, buoyed up by his care. When we feel like our world is crashing down around us, like waves engulfing us, God is near, an anchor in the storm and a beacon of hope in the waves.

Just as the sea's expanse is a mystery to our human understanding, we also cannot fathom the height, depth or breadth of God's love for us. We are unable to fully grasp the enormity of a love that stretches further than the horizon and the sea that appears to go on forever. There is no end to God's amazing grace and love. The almighty creator, who placed the moon in the heavens and set the tides in motion, cares about you and the prayers and hopes of your heart.

The words of the hymn 'How great thou art' capture wonderfully the sense of awe and praise we feel when we behold nature at its most dramatic; our souls cannot help but cry out in worship. The lyrics began life as poem set to a Swedish melody, in 1885, inspired by a sudden thunderstorm, followed by a calm sea.

God's love doesn't change; it remains firm in even the fiercest storms we face. We can know hope for the future, though it feels lost beneath the waves that overwhelm us. The impossible becomes possible when we trust in God. He is with us in all the highs and lows of life and our struggles can be turned to triumph and joy, like the changing of the tides, when we commit them to God.

 Reflect

When the waves crash, know that the Lord remains in control. He is the hope we can cling to, our anchor when the waves roll. Give thanks to God for his constancy and bring to him any storms you are facing.

The same God who directs the waves that crash against rocks or harbour walls is in the gentle lapping waves, washing languidly on the shore. Recall times in your life when God has been close in the crashing waves of life, calming the storms within you.

 Pray

Turner of tides, your majesty is displayed in the waves that rise powerfully and as they lap gently on the shore. I speak your name over my battles, the waves that rise. May they break and retreat, as you make a way to smoother seas ahead. Help me to remember that you are with me in the storms, my anchor and safe harbour. Amen.

34

Legend of the sand dollar

> **M**ay the God of hope fill you with all joy and peace as you trust in him, so that you may overflow with hope by the power of the Holy Spirit.
> ROMANS 15:13

We walked along the beach with my dad's cousin, near her home on the central Californian coastline. We found among the sand many treasures washed up on the beach: shells and beautiful sea glass, of green, blue and white, formed into smooth and frosted pebbles by the waves and sands of the Pacific Ocean. But the greatly anticipated finds were the white, sun-bleached urchin shells, known as sand dollars, something we could never find on our beaches in England. I was thrilled to see these curiosities in real life, scattered by the sea along the beach.

Sand dollars are burrowing sea urchins which get their name from their similarity in appearance to large silver coins after they have been bleached by the sun when they wash up on shore. These beautiful porcelain-like shells, which are very fragile, have a symbolic story to tell.

A legend tells how these creatures represent the story of Christ, with a star on the top of their shell that reminds us of the star of Bethlehem that led the magi to the Christ child. Around this is the outline of an Easter lily, symbolic of Jesus' resurrection from the grave, like a lily bursting forth in bloom, so that we may know life everlasting. When the sand dollar is turned over, we see on the other side markings resembling a poinsettia, the Christmas flower. Thus both the birth and resurrection of our Saviour are depicted.

When it is broken, emerging from within the sand dollar are five tiny, white bird shapes, like doves. These are actually teeth, used by the creature during its lifetime, which float loose inside the shell when it dries out. Some people believe this symbolises releasing peace into the world, with doves representing the Holy Spirit in the Bible and often depicted in art as symbols of peace, hope and goodwill. Just like the sand dollar being cracked open to release these 'doves', Jesus' body was broken for us. His resurrection made the way for us to receive a peace that goes beyond human understanding.

How incredible that the story of Christ's sacrifice, his victory over death and God's redemption plan can be seen etched into the sand dollar. Sharing our story, the times we have known an inner peace through trusting in Jesus when circumstances were difficult, can be a great witness to others. Just like the disciples were given the great commission to share the good news of Jesus, we too can be part of spreading God's peace in the world.

 Reflect

Which part of the legend of the sand dollar stood out to you? Spend some time reflecting on this, prayerfully meditating on what God is saying through this.

How might you be called to spread peace in the world? What difference can you make in your home, community or in the wider world?

Pray

God of peace, how awe-inspiring it is to consider the story of your love for humankind. I join in with the joy of the angels to celebrate your birth and give thanks for your rising in glory. Help me to speak peace, that others might tell your story and know peace unending. Amen.

35

Birdsong

'The Lord your God in your midst, The Mighty One, will save; He will rejoice over you with gladness, He will quiet *you* with His love, He will rejoice over you with singing.'
ZEPHANIAH 3:17 (NKJV)

The symphony of sounds created by birds hidden from view above our heads can be heard when walking through woodlands or tree-lined walkways. This melody can often only be truly appreciated when we pause and step away from the usual distractions and bustle of life. It is only when we stop and listen that we fully hear birdsong. If we close our eyes, sounds of nature can flood our senses. Birdsong is joined in glorious harmony by bees and perhaps the distant noise of sheep, the sounds of nature seeming to get suddenly louder, as we key into the melodies carried on the breeze.

In spring or early summer, it is easier to hear birdsong, when nests are full of fledglings and their parent birds are noisily protecting them from local cats and other creatures that may threaten them. But birdsong goes on all year round, if we listen carefully, with the intensity of the melody and the species of birds joining the throng varying depending on the hour of the day or the time of year.

To hear the song that God sings over us, we need to pause and listen. Many other distractions and sounds compete for our attention, yet if we listen for his voice, it will ring out, like the clearest of birdsongs. It may be a gentle whisper, like in the calling of Samuel (1 Samuel 3), a nudging in our being or a simple phrase that falls into our heart. We need at times to step away from the noise and chaos and listen for God's still, small voice.

If we are honest about the voices we listen to, we might admit that the voices of regret or failure, telling us we are not enough or not worthy, can resound loudest in our ears and hearts. But God sings over us a song of redemption, forgiveness and freedom that can drown out the words we have too long believed are true, if we stop and listen.

Just as there are seasons when it is easier to hear birdsong, you might recall times in your faith journey when you more clearly heard the song God was singing over you. Sometimes it seems he is silent or the song less audible above the noise. In the same way that we need to be beside someone to hear them whisper, might you need to invite the Lord to draw near or step closer to him?

What might God be speaking to you about, if you listen for that still, small voice? Maybe he wants to remind you of a time in the past when he sung over you with joy or to let you know for the first time that he rejoices over you with song. Reflect on times when you've heard his voice clearly in the past and been inspired listening to the sound of nature, as a reminder that God sings over you.

Reflect

Could you take some time to step outside into nature? Create space to stop for a moment and hear birdsong. Soak in the sounds and give thanks for the incredible song we hear in nature and from God.

How can you find quiet to focus and really listen for his voice, to hear the song he sings over you or the gentle whisper?

Pray

Lord God, help my restless heart in need of stillness and peace. Grant me opportunity to pause and listen for your song. May I tune in to the words you sing over me, your promises and the love that surrounds me, if I only take the time to rest in your presence. Amen.

36

The passion flower

> For God so loved the world that he gave his one and only Son, that whoever believes in him shall not perish but have eternal life. For God did not send his Son into the world to condemn the world, but to save the world through him.
> JOHN 3:16–17

In July 2000, for the first time in their long history, the York Mystery Plays were staged inside the incredible setting of York Minster, in a large-scale performance to mark the new millennium. I was fortunate to share the experience of witnessing this moving and awe-inspiring dramatic scriptural depiction with my mum.

Originally called the York Corpus Christi Plays, the York Mystery Plays are a cycle of 48 plays or pageants that cover sacred biblical history from the creation to the last judgement, traditionally performed outside in the city of York from the mid-14th century until they were suppressed in 1569. In the modern revivals, professional actors always play the role of Jesus, with the large ensemble cast often comprising many local amateurs. Ian McShane played Lucifer in 1963, and Judi Dench performed in the plays before she became a professional actor. Seeing the crucifixion of Christ portrayed in front of our eyes, the actor lifted on a wooden cross in the centre of the magnificent historic place of worship, really brought home what Jesus endured. It was heart-wrenching to watch in the flesh.

In the 1600s Spanish Christian missionaries spoke of an eye-catching purple-and-green flower, the unique structure of which they saw as representing key moments in Jesus' crucifixion. The passion flower has five petals and five sepals that together represent the ten faithful apostles of Christ. The radial filament or corona reminds us of the crown of thorns he bore for our sins, and the five anthers tell of the Saviour's wounds to his hands, feet and side. Leaves that grow around the flower have three points, thought to signify the Holy Trinity.

The passion flower contains within its beauty symbols of the truth that Jesus broke the chains of sin and shame and was pierced for our transgression, so that we might live in freedom. The nails he surrendered to are starkly depicted in the central stigmas, yet we can rejoice that he rose again. The regal purple of the flower recognises his kingship and authority over death itself.

Reflecting on Jesus' sacrifice represented in this flower, we can meditate on his resurrection power. He demonstrated a grace so amazing, securing for us a love unending, compassion unfailing and life everlasting. Because of this we can know joy despite the trials, hope in the heartache, comfort despite the pain and peace in the storms. Whatever life brings, we are sustained by grace and held by the hand of God.

Reflect

Meditate on the powerful messages of the passion flower: growing within a garden, the truth of the cross – the key to salvation and everlasting life.

Spend a moment to reflect on the truth that Jesus thought you were worth dying for. He loves you and would have done it even if you were the only person on earth. Give thanks for the sacrifice Jesus made.

Pray

Christ in your passion, your death and resurrection purchased for all humankind a grace we do not deserve. I can let go of shame in the light of your love not defined by my mistakes, the hurts I have received or the voices of others. I can live life to the full because of your great love. Amen.

37

Lessons from the butterfly

> Do not conform to the pattern of this world, but be transformed by the renewing of your mind. Then you will be able to test and approve what God's will is – his good, pleasing and perfect will.
> ROMANS 12:2

I sat in Birmingham Cathedral, seeking some quiet time to pray and reflect. Before and behind me were the beautiful stained-glass windows created by the famous pre-Raphaelite artist Edward Burne-Jones and William Morris. However, as I closed my eyes, I became very aware of the noises that occupied the corners of this usually quiet place of contemplation. Sounds of crucial flooring repairs being done and the prayers of the man sitting alongside another person on my right-hand side.

My initial frustration at these sounds gave way to a thought. If people did not lift their voice to pray for others, this place would not be serving the needs of the community. If the peace of this place was not interrupted by this momentary, necessary, building maintenance, it could not so effectively continue to offer a welcome in the days and years to come.

The Victorian artistry of the stained-glass windows had been concealed while undergoing cleaning and restoration in 2023, to retain their fortitude against the elements. We are all in need of restoration or repair at times, to be sustained and continue to flourish. Interruptions, changes of plans or being broken by ill health can be frustrating and disheartening. Yet it is part of life's journey and is needed in some seasons for us to develop and be made whole again. Like the Kintsugi method of mending broken pottery, where the fractured parts are not hidden but fixed with decorative gold, it is a visible reminder of embracing imperfection, celebrating flaws and restoration.

Butterflies go through stages of metamorphosis, achieving their wings by going through a time of brokenness and transformation. We all have a testimony about the ways we have been rebuilt, changed and renewed by our experiences. You are allowed to be a masterpiece and a work in progress at the same time. God makes all things new, but we often endure a time of refining before we are transformed.

I have long been heartened by all that butterflies can teach us about the power of hope. They are a symbol of new beginnings, proof that it is possible to overcome darkness and be transformed. We all have our own stories of deliverance and reliance on God for transformation that can encourage others, in times when hope seems frail.

How might we acknowledge our caterpillar and chrysalis selves as part of our story? What could we be learning if we feel that this is where we are now? Transforming our minds might be a daily decision, perhaps the work of a lifetime, but we can be renewed daily when we rely on the God of transformation.

Reflect

Time is needed for transformation to happen, renewing our mindset cannot be done in a moment. Bring to God those areas of your life where you need help to change.

Just as the process of a butterfly's metamorphosis is unseen, consider the changes God has made in your heart and mind. Even on days when you feel like a caterpillar again, know there is no turning back.

Pray

God of new beginnings, thank you that the butterfly reminds me that beauty can come from brokenness. Help me to trust in you to transform me daily and renew my mind. Even in times of darkness, may I trust afresh in your plan for my life. I am not who I was. Amen.

38

Turning towards the Son

> Let us fix our eyes on Jesus, the author and perfecter of our faith, who for the joy set before Him endured the cross, scorning its shame, and sat down at the right hand of the throne of God.
> HEBREWS 12:2 (BSB)

Like many families, we have grown sunflowers in our garden, watching to see which one will grow tallest. They reach incredible heights to get as close as possible to the sun, leaning towards the source of light that helps them to grow and flourish. When visiting the sunflower meadow at our local farm, we have seen each of the countless sunflowers across a vast field; their distinctive faces with petals like golden rays of the sun, all turning in the same direction. Following the source of their strength and vitality, maximising the amount of life-giving brightness they can absorb.

Sunflowers display heliotropism, meaning they follow the path of the sun during the day. Incredibly, they do this by making a subtle change to their rate of growth, first on one side and then on the other, so that they lean towards the sun as it moves. Only young sunflowers do this, using a natural circadian rhythm to garner the most light for photosynthesis. Mature sunflowers mainly face the east, the direction of the rising sun.

In the same way that sunflowers turn towards the sun, we find we grow and are strengthened the more we turn towards the Son: Jesus the light of life. Plants need light to photosynthesise, so it's only natural that they would do their best to get closer to their source of sunlight. Are you drawing near to the Son, getting enough light to help you thrive and grow in your faith? We need to transfer our gaze away from other things that have taken our attention away from him, to turn fully towards Jesus. Looking away from other distractions that do not fulfil our need for sustenance, we need to keep reaching towards the source of our strength and growth, Jesus the Son.

There is something lovely about feeling the warmth of sunlight touching our face. Naturally rejuvenating, sunlight is a source of vitamin D that has health benefits and can lift our mood. Basking in the light of God's love can be transformational, bringing light to our days and a source of strength and salvation.

God wants to see many faces fix their eyes upon Jesus, seeking his face and looking to him as the light of life, for guidance and strength to sustain and brighten our lives. May we return to God for our every need and point others to the source of our strength and hope, keeping our eyes fixed on him, turning towards the Son.

 Reflect

In order to turn fully towards Jesus, what might you need to look away from? Consider what is turning your head, taking your focus away from God.

What might you need to change or prioritise to spend more time in God's presence, like the sunflower adapting to get the full benefit of sunny daylight hours?

Pray

Source of my strength, may I keep reaching towards you, the Son, light of the world. Help me to continually fix my eyes on you and follow you daily. Lord, I pray for others to turn towards the light of life that only you can supply, which does not fade with the setting sun. Amen.

39

His eye is on the sparrow

> Look at the birds of the air; they do not sow or reap or store away in barns, and yet your heavenly Father feeds them.
> MATTHEW 6:26

When visiting my maternal grandparents, we would always take our newest treasured items to show them. During my teenage years, I remember sharing with them my latest CD, an EP released by my favourite band at the time. One of the songs was a modern reworking of the song 'His Eye is on the Sparrow'. It is the only time I can remember hearing my Nanny sing, apart from when she was hanging out washing in the garden, wearing a summer dress with white flowers on, which always reminded me of clouds in a blue summer sky. She sang what I had not realised was a well-known song, written in praise of God, long before a 1990s girl band with gospel roots reimagined it.

The song was originally written by Civilla Martin, inspired by scripture and the words of a dear friend she visited in New York in 1906. The Doolittles were a couple who knew much hardship and physical limitations yet were able to bring comfort and inspiration to those who knew them. Upon asking how they could remain so hopeful, Mrs Doolittle replied: 'His eye is on the sparrow, and I know he watches me.' Civilla spoke of the 'beauty of this simple expression of boundless faith' and the hymn was the outcome of that conversation.

God cares for all that he made, however small or insignificant they may seem. He is concerned about the details of your life, just as he knows each sparrow that falls. We often fail to notice the many birds that live around us, hidden from view in trees or flying in the skies above. They remain unobserved, as we go busily about our day, except when we see a fallen bird or when an errant cat carries one into our home. Yet the Bible tells us that not a single bird, animal or plant goes unnoticed by creator God.

Sparrows are mentioned several times in scripture, symbolising God's care and provision for his creation, the importance of humility, and the fact that even seemingly insignificant creatures are known and loved by God. Though they are birds considered to be not of great worth, they are valued and seen by God, just as he sees and loves you. As Matthew 10:29–31 explains: 'Are not two sparrows sold for a penny? Yet not one of them will fall to the ground outside your Father's care. And even the very hairs of your head are all numbered. So don't be afraid; you are worth more than many sparrows.'

The creator of the universe, which stretches further than any human has ever been able to navigate or measure, also cares for every tiny bird and for each of us. Despite how insignificant we may feel, compared to the hugeness of the world, the scriptures tell us that God knows every hair on your head just as he sees every sparrow and is watching over you in all seasons.

Reflect

Do you need to believe afresh that God provides for you when you bring any request to him?

You are valuable, the God who sees each sparrow that falls is interested in you. If you find this hard to believe, take time to bring these feelings to God and know he is with you in all that you are facing.

Pray

Lord of all creation, you are so magnificent, yet you care about each one of us. The earth trembles at your name, yet you care for each tiny sparrow that falls. Thank you that you see and know me and you lavish gentleness and compassion on all that you made. Amen.

40

At the close of the day

> The sun rises and the sun sets, and hurries back to where it rises.
> ECCLESIASTES 1:5

Life is filled with beginnings and endings. Existence itself is bookended by these inevitable opposites. Each new sunrise could not happen if the sun had not set on the day gone by. There are times when we can see a purpose in an ending; other times it is hard to accept a season is over or a person has left us. God paints the sky with beautiful colours as the sun goes down, and we can feel a sense of wonder at how it is different every night and across the seasons, yet it never fails to happen.

I am sure like me you have seen some amazing sunsets, over the sea, dipping below the hills or disappearing behind the familiar view of gardens or houses seen from the window of your home. When visiting Key West in Florida, we were delighted to see the sunset celebration that happens every night in Mallory Square. Artists and performers gather, weather permitting, to share in the profound joy that comes from witnessing together one of nature's most stunning spectacles.

In an array of varying light and colours, there is a different display each night – pinks, purples, gold or red filling the sky, as the sun descends below the horizon. Sunset reassures us that the God who paints the sky with colour is with us at the close of the day. There is a sense of pervading calm about sunset; the day drawing to a close can feel comforting. Whatever has gone before, the day is done, whether it has been a day of triumph and productivity or a day of difficulty and trials. We can reflect on the day, as we draw the curtains or close the blinds.

Though the falling of night and encroaching darkness can be associated with fear or negativity, I've always felt that with evening and the setting of the sun comes a comforting cosiness. Knowing that the day's work is done, all that is passed has gone and there is always a fresh start preparing to dawn. Sunset brings a sense of closure and time to rest before the new day dawns, bringing its own challenges and triumphs.

Reflect

Spend some time remembering sunsets you have seen. Perhaps look back at photos, reliving the joy of witnessing the incredible beauty at the end of a day. Give thanks for the faithfulness of God, day after day.

Bring to God the challenges, changes or joys of the day. If you need to find peace at the close of a difficult day, rest in the knowledge that he goes before us and beside us into whatever tomorrow brings.

Pray

Painter of every sunset, you are there in the sunrise, which awakens the sky with colour and light, and you are with me at the close of the day. Lord, help me to take forward into tomorrow the joys and learning, leaving behind mistakes or frustrations of today, like the dew that evaporates with the rising sun. Amen.

Epilogue

It is my hope that you have found this book encouraging, in whatever season you are journeying through. I pray that you have found fresh inspiration in reading these reflections and meditating on the accompanying artwork.

Where the reflection points have challenged you, may you continue to pray and seek God in your daily life. Perhaps it has inspired you to pause and ponder the wonders of creation that surround us and speak of God's majesty and love. I encourage you to find space to immerse yourself in nature and notice the beauty in every season, as it unfolds. Take time to listen for the prompting of the Lord, that still, small voice, and seek him anew. Observe the sights, sounds and fragrances of the created world, a world that reflects his grace and glory.

Perhaps you will revisit these reflections in the coming seasons, asking God to reveal himself afresh through nature. Take time to listen for his words, the song he wants to sing over you or the prompting to act or pray. May you find rest beneath his wings, strength for the day and keep looking for the stars in even the darkest of skies.

Leading the reader through 30 selected psalms, the Revd Clare Hayns and her son Micah capture the essence of this ancient text – the worship, the grieving and the joy – and open up new ways to engage with its riches. There is also a playlist of suggested music to accompany the reflections.

Garden Song
Exploring the psalms through paintings, reflections and prayers
Reflections by Clare Hayns, artwork by Micah Hayns
978 1 80039 237 3 £14.99
brfonline.org.uk

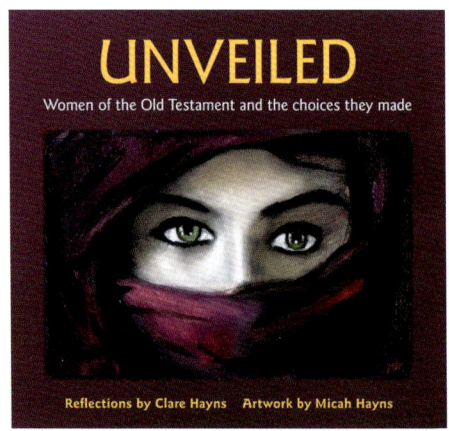

Some women of the Hebrew Bible are well known; many others are barely remembered. Even when they are, we often don't think about what we might learn from them. Written with frankness and humour and illustrated with striking artwork, *Unveiled* explores the stories of 40 women in 40 days.

Unveiled
Women of the Old Testament and the choices they made
Reflections by Clare Hayns, artwork by Micah Hayns
978 1 80039 072 0 £14.99
brfonline.org.uk

A 40-day journey exploring the themes of hope and new life through vivid biblical images, *Holding Onto Hope* can be used through Lent or during any 40-day period.

Holding Onto Hope
40 days of God's encouragement through art and reflections
Amy Boucher Pye and Leo Boucher
978 1 80039 200 7 £12.99
brfonline.org.uk

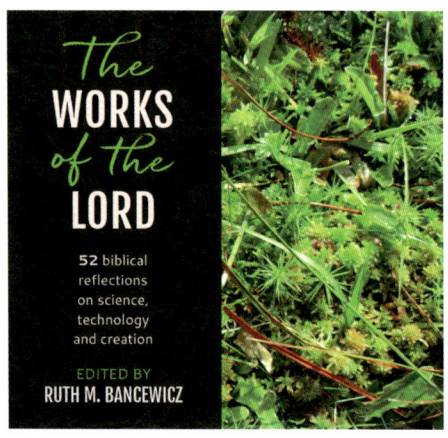

We all benefit from science, and we all make choices about how to use its fruits. This series of reflections, written by a diverse group of scientists and theologians, lets scientific discoveries fuel your worship and helps you to consider how we can move forward wisely in a scientific society.

The Works of the Lord
52 biblical reflections on science, technology and creation
Edited by Ruth M. Bancewicz
978 1 80039 285 4 £12.99
brfonline.org.uk

Inspiring people of all ages to grow in Christian faith

BRF Ministries is the home of Anna Chaplaincy, Living Faith, Messy Church and Parenting for Faith

As a charity, our work would not be possible without fundraising and gifts in wills. To find out more and to donate, visit brf.org.uk/give or call +44 (0)1235 462305

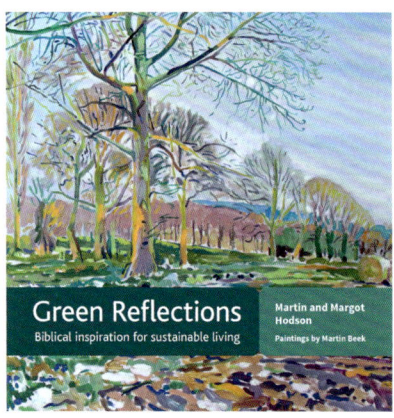

How should we look after the world we inhabit? Martin and Margot Hodson bring together scientific and theological wisdom to offer 62 reflections inspired by scripture passages in a thoughtful exploration that encourages both reflection and response.

Green Reflections
Biblical inspiration for sustainable living
Martin and Margot Hodson with paintings by Martin Beek
978 1 80039 068 3 £8.99
brfonline.org.uk